THE EUCHARISTIC SPRINGTIME

THE EUCHARISTIC SPRINGTIME

The Eucharistic Springtime

BY

Fr Sean Davidson

SAINT CARLO PRESS

NIHIL OBSTAT
Rev. Paul Chandler, Ph.D.

IMPRIMATUR
✠ Most Reverend Peter Murphy, STD
Bishop of Armidale
15 October 2025

Saint Carlo Press © 2026

For information, visit:
www.stcarloaustralia.com

ISBN
978-1-7645453-0-3

CONTENTS

INTRODUCTION

Whenever we contemplate a mystery of our faith it is always important to trace its origins back to the Scriptures and the sacred Tradition which comes to us from Christ and his apostles. In the early Church, the Eucharist was so important that it was seen as Christ's primary will and testament bequeathed to the world. In the first centuries of Christianity, before the books of the New Testament were clearly defined, when people spoke of the New Testament, they were referring primarily to the mystery of the Eucharist. The New Testament was a sacrament before it was a document.[1] The inspired books which were finally approved as belonging to what we call the authentic New Testament were the books that had been read in the context of the "New Testament" of the Eucharistic sacrifice. All of this is explained in detail by Doctor Scott Hahn in his excellent work entitled, *Consuming the Word.*

I include this truth in the introduction to this book in order to make it clear that Scripture is intrinsically related to Christ's gift of the Eucharist. The Eucharist is not some "add-on" to divine

1   Scott Hahn, *Consuming the Word* (New York: Image, 2013) p.39.

revelation provided by the Catholic Church. The Eucharist is central to divine revelation itself. The Old Testament contained many prefigurations of the Eucharistic mystery. All generations of Christians after the age of the apostles were always destined by Christ to meet him in the flesh only through the Most Blessed Sacrament. Jesus was born in Bethlehem, which means "House of Bread" and laid in a manger, which comes from the French verb "to eat." It was ordained by God from all eternity that his Son should come into our world to become for all generations the Bread of Life.

Only when the Eucharistic body of Christ is present on a hundred thousand altars all around the globe is the goal of the Incarnation complete. The Lord himself explained this to his disciples in the sixth chapter of the Gospel of John. He made it clear that he had come in order to give us his flesh to be the nourishment of that divinisation which he would begin in Baptism. We will commence our meditations on the Eucharistic mystery with a reminder of what transpired on that monumental day upon which Christ boldly proclaimed the truth of the Eucharist in the synagogue of Capernaum. It was a revelation for all ages, as well as an advance catechesis that he provided for his closest friends one year before their first Holy Communion.

The Bread of Life in the Gospel of John

We recall the familiar scene. Jesus and his apostles had been working hard for almost two years to spread the Good News throughout the region of Galilee. Wherever Christ's sacred footsteps passed, there were miracles, healings, resurrections from the dead, and souls set on fire by the words of light which poured forth from his lips. Excited crowds came to hear him speak in their hundreds and even in their thousands. Christ, whose every heartbeat was an act of purest love, was able to handle the constant self-giving for souls which had become his daily bread. However, his poor apostles were by now worn out by the intensity of this existence. The Lord, in his merciful concern for both their spiritual and their human well-being, observed that they needed a break. He invited them to come apart and rest for a while in a lonely place near the north shore of Lake Galilee. Yet, the rest was to be a short one, for the crowds had discovered their location and soon came like hungry sheep in search of their Shepherd.

Deeply moved by the thought of their broken lives in this valley of tears, as well as their unfulfilled desire for happiness, the Shepherd welcomed this interruption of his rest and began to teach the crowds at length (Mark 6:34). He would gladly accept the opportunity to teach them the path of true happiness. It is unlikely that the apostles were as eager to welcome the interruption, but they had long since learned to live with such things.

As evening began to fall, Christ asked his disciples how they would find earthly food to complement the spiritual nourishment he had just provided for his flock. He asked this not because he was ignorant of anything, but so as to test the generosity of his friends and to prepare them for a stunning revelation of divine providence. More than a revelation of the superabundant generosity of God he was also planning to work this Eucharistic sign in the wilderness as the prelude to his sermon on the Bread of Life just hours later. All that happens in the sixth chapter of the Gospel of John is related to the revelation of the Eucharistic mystery. The apostles eventually brought before him a generous little benefactor who was willing to part with his own store of food so that at least some in the crowds might have something to eat (John 6:9).

The boy's act of human generosity was precisely what the divine generosity had been waiting for. Christ gave thanks to the Father for the child's five loaves and two fish, then handed a small portion of this meager supply to each of his apostles who began to distribute it to the crowds. The apostles soon discovered that the more they drew from the small amount of food that they were carrying in their sacks, the more they seemed to be carrying. In the end, thousands of souls had eaten their fill, and there was enough left over to fill twelve baskets to the brim. One can almost picture the joy on the face of the generous child who unwittingly found himself at the heart of this divine prodigy.

The crowds were elated to say the least. Not only did they have food in abundance, but they saw in this sign the kind of wonder they associated with the Messianic era (John 6:14). Immediately they started to proclaim that the kingly prophet, that is the Messiah, had finally arrived. Plans for the announcement of this great news to Jerusalem were soon being formulated (John 6:15). Christ, understanding the misguided nature of their zealous desire for an earthly king, was not moved by their messianic fervour, but rather dismissed the crowds and retreated into the mountains for a time of silent prayer. Thus, do we learn how to deal with praise and excitement that are merely human. His own apostles were instructed to go to their boat and wait. If he had not arrived by nightfall, they were to cross the lake to Capernaum and wait for him there.

Jesus preceded his monumental sermon on the Bread of Life with a night of silent contemplation on the mountaintop. At about 3am, the fourth watch of the night, the apostles found themselves struggling against a high wind on the waters of Lake Galilee (Matthew 14:25). In the shadows of the night they then made out a white figure drawing near to the boat. Terrified, they cried out in panic, but discovered that from the white figure came a familiar voice. It was Christ himself, walking on the water, clearly demonstrating his power over the laws of nature, just before he proclaimed to them the unfathomable wonder of the Bread of Life. "Be not afraid, I AM!" is the literal translation of what Jesus called out to his friends from the stormy waters (John 6:20). Pronouncing the divine name in relation to himself just before his sermon on the Bread of Life suggests that before one can believe in the Eucharist one must first understand that Christ is God made flesh. Thus, he has the power to accomplish whatever he wills. As soon as he entered the boat, peace came with him, and the apostles fell at his feet in adoration (Matthew 14:33).

A Sermon with Curious Consequences

Day soon dawns, and so begins a morning of miracles, before the apostles finally find themselves in the synagogue of Capernaum at the feet of the Master (Mark 6:53-56, John 6:24). Some of the crowds that had experienced the sign of the multiplication of the loaves, eventually found their way back to Capernaum, and once there, they heard that Christ was now teaching in the synagogue. Perplexed as to how he had managed to return to the village, when he clearly had not boarded any of the boats that left the shore the evening before, many of them ran to find him. (John 6:25) As they entered into the synagogue's prayerful atmosphere, no doubt breathless and unable to think clearly for excitement, Jesus knew that the time had come to unveil the truth about his mission; even if this would inevitably put an end to the fervour that would have soon spread like wildfire throughout the land. A conversation on the manna from heaven ensues.

Those present had rightly recognised the parallel between Moses feeding the crowds in the wilderness and what Jesus had done the day before. He had accomplished something that at least resembled one of the signs which would be associated with the Messiah. Yet Moses had actually made the bread fall from the skies, and they would be satisfied if Jesus could do something similar so as to remove all shadow of doubt from their minds. Jesus interjected to correct an error. Moses was a mere mortal;

it was God the Father who had caused the manna to rain down from the heavens (John 6:32). Yet those who ate that ancient manna did not receive eternal life from it. God the Father had far greater designs upon the age which would witness the coming of his Son. A new Bread from Heaven was to be rained down upon the world each day, and this Bread would bring eternal life to those who eat it.

The crowds were delighted to hear about this glorious new manna, until they learned that the Bread from Heaven is Jesus himself. He who has descended into the world from the heavenly realms announced that he will find a way of offering his very flesh and blood to human beings as their food. The delight suddenly turned to horror. Those present in the synagogue found themselves faced with two stumbling-blocks, and the second was more shocking than the first. Not only does a man who spent most of his whole life in Nazareth as a carpenter say that he has somehow come down from heaven, but that they must also eat his flesh and drink his blood. There could be no doubt about the literal meaning of this second stumbling-block because when he was given the opportunity to recant or clarify it, he insisted upon it all the more forcefully.

The previously excited crowds now began to murmur against him and to dispute with each other about the shocking nature of his words. One after another, they began to depart from the synagogue in disgust, no longer sure of what to make of one who would say such intolerable things (John 6:60). They wanted an earthly king who would be wise enough to outwit the Romans, powerful enough to banish the enemy from the land altogether, and prodigious enough to find ways of filling their stomachs with an abundance of earthly bread each day. Instead, they were offered a King of a Eucharistic Kingdom who desires to take up his reign of love in hearts and communicate his divine immortality to souls with supernatural food.

With this one sermon, Christ threw away the possibility of an earthly kind of kingship in favour of a Eucharistic Kingship. The worldly minds of those in the crowd had no interest in talk of mysterious supernatural kingships or in the eternal benefits he was promising to bestow, but only in those that are material and plain to the eyes. After almost two years of witnessing great ministerial success, the apostles looked on downcast as Jesus lost the Galilean crowds forever. Not only did he let them depart without protest, but he even asked the apostles if they also wish to depart (John 6:67). The decisive moment in his public ministry had arrived. Only those who accepted his teaching on the Bread of Life could continue to journey with him.

Saint Peter and the Eucharist

In that synagogue of Capernaum, as it became clear to the disciples that Jesus was not interested in winning over large crowds to a compromised version of the truth, and that faithful Christians would only ever be a remnant, another deep spiritual truth was revealed. As Jesus asked his closest friends if they also wanted to leave him, it was Saint Peter alone who responded. With great loyalty to Christ, he boldly proclaimed that the apostles were going nowhere (John 6:68). They had seen Jesus walk on water, they had come to know and love his adorable Person, and they would continue to stand faithfully by his side. If he said that they must eat his flesh and drink his blood, then he said it for a good reason, and although they could not understand it, they would accept that the Holy One could only ever address them words of life and truth. "He forbade us to tell lies; still less will he himself tell a lie. Nothing is impossible for God except to tell a lie."[1]

Peter knew that the one thing of which Jesus was incapa-

1   Saint Clement of Rome, *Letter to the Corinthians.*

ble was falsehood; and so, they would accept what he said on good faith, giving his trustworthiness the benefit of the doubt, over their own limited way of understanding. This is the perfect Eucharistic attitude. Like Saint Peter in Capernaum, we believe in the Real Presence without understanding it because we trust in the Person of Jesus and his words of purest truth. Every day, in spite of the dullness of our understanding, we renew our faith in the words of the one who said, "This is my body" and not "This symbolises my body." Such acts of faith are very meritorious and daily bring an increase to our glory in heaven.

Not only does Peter offer us the perfect Eucharistic attitude, but there is something deeper at work in this mysterious moment in Capernaum. There is a reason why it is Peter who comes to Christ's defence and who professes in the name of the apostolic group the first fruits of Eucharistic faith. Only that little flock which is represented by Peter, who himself will soon be made chief shepherd of Christ's sheep, stays faithful to Christ in Capernaum. We can see in this a symbol for the fact that only the little flock which remains in full communion with the successor of Saint Peter will be able to stay faithful to the Eucharistic mystery. Only those united to the pope and under his authority will continue to grow in faith and love for the Blessed Sacrament. The Catholic Church has never ceased to press forward into an ever deeper understanding of the Eucharistic mystery. "The essential commitment and, above all, the visible grace and source of supernatural strength for the Church as the People of God is to persevere and advance constantly in Eucharistic life and Eucharistic piety and to develop spiritually in the climate of the Eucharist."[1]

Catholics who separate themselves from the pope can expect at best a stagnant form of devotion to the Eucharist and at worst a total loss of Eucharistic faith. An external façade of devotion may

[1]   Pope John Paul II, *Redemptor Hominis* §20.

remain for a while, but soon it will begin to disintegrate, fossilise, or tend towards extremes. This truth never shone more clearly than it did in the heresies and schisms which tore at the Mystical Body of Christ in the sixteenth century. Soon the "reformers" themselves were involved in fierce disputes with one another about the mystery of the Eucharist. Eventually, hundreds of different theories about the meaning of the celebration of the "Lord's Supper" would be created. Without the pope, what was meant to be the Sacrament of Unity soon became the source of division.

In addition to the protective and unifying force of the charism of Peter, we also have need of the Church's magisterium in order to nourish and deepen our understanding of the Eucharist. It was Peter whose voice rang out in fidelity to Christ in the synagogue of Capernaum, and whose voice still proclaims the pure truth about the most holy Sacrament of the Altar. The popes are given a special grace to enlighten our minds about this mystery, and so in pondering their teachings, we can receive an increase of Eucharistic understanding as well as a strengthening of faith.

Throughout the course of this work, I would like to make use of an insight provided by Pope Saint John Paul II in order to enter more deeply into this mystery. It comes from his first encyclical, *Redemptor Hominis,* which contained a short but enlightening teaching on the Sacrament of the Eucharist. He wrote: "With all the greater reason, then, it is not permissible for us, in thought, life or action, to take away from this truly most holy Sacrament its full magnitude and its essential meaning. It is at one and the same time a *Sacrifice-Sacrament, a Communion-Sacrament, and a Presence-Sacrament.* And, although it is true that the Eucharist always was and must continue to be the most profound revelation of the human brotherhood of Christ's disciples and confessors, it cannot be treated merely as an "occasion" for manifesting this brotherhood."[2]

2   Pope John Paul II, *Redemptor Hominis,* §20. Emphasis added.

In this final statement the Pope is condemning the sad and erroneous tendency which was present in some quarters of the post-conciliar Church to downplay the mysterious dimensions of the Sacrament of the Eucharist and treat it as nothing more than a fraternal meal. This mindset which was actively promoted by some liturgists and pastors, along with the spiritual cancer of irreverence which was its consequence, led to an unprecedented loss of true Eucharistic faith in many Catholics. This tendency was often motivated by a misguided sacramental theology as well as a false spirit of ecumenism which would seek to hasten unity with our separated brethren at the price of trying to hide the full truth of what we believe. True ecumenism is a priority for all Christians but it is the fruit of a patient, honest dialogue, and not a denial of the truth. Instead of attaining unity with those outside the Catholic Church, all that this false brand of ecumenism attained was a new division within the heart of the Catholic Church.

Pope Saint John Paul II was determined to bring the sons and daughters of the Church back to true Eucharistic faith and devotion. It was his goal to bring us back to an awareness of what he called the "full magnitude" of the mystery. The key which he provided in order to unlock the secret of the Sacrament is found in the following statement: "It is at one and the same time a Sacrifice-Sacrament, a Communion-Sacrament, and a Presence-Sacrament." The Eucharist comprises three different dimensions, each of which brings its own particular grace and from which we can draw each day if we are correctly disposed. The word sacrament was initially a translation of the Greek word mystery. The Eucharist is a mystery of sacrifice, a mystery of communion, and a mystery of divine presence.

The bulk of this book will consist of an attempt to unpack this one great truth which the saintly pontiff provided for us at the outset of his papal ministry. We will ponder each of these three dimensions of the Eucharist in the order determined by the pope and with a view to bringing our lives into conformity with this teaching. From the Blessed Sacrament there flows through the world an unseen torrent of divine life. This torrent transforms all those souls who learn how to live in a way that draws deeply from the fullness of grace available in these three dimensions of the one great Sacrament of Love. How sad it will be on Judgment Day for all who spurn the Eucharistic fountain of life, and who only then discover that by means of all the grace that was available to them they could have become saints. The words that Jesus once addressed to a great Eucharistic saint are addressed to us all: "My Heart is overflowing with graces intended for souls. Bring them to my Eucharistic Heart."[1]

---

1 Dina Bélanger, *The Autobiography of Dina Bélanger.* (Quebec, Atelier Rouge, 1995) p.342.

I

A SACRIFICE-SACRAMENT

One New Sacrifice

The Old Covenant had many different sacrifices. Some were offered to God in adoration, some in thanksgiving, some in reparation for sins, and some in supplication of his gifts. The New Covenant has only one saving sacrifice, that of the Cross. It is the cause of grace and forgiveness. At the Last Supper, Jesus joined the shedding of his blood for the remission of sins to a sacrificial liturgical rite, and made this rite the centre of his New Covenant. "This *chalice* which is poured out for you *is the new covenant* in my blood" (Luke 22:20). What took place on Good Friday is inseparable from what took place on Holy Thursday and we can say that Calvary was itself Eucharistic because of its connection to what took place the evening before at the Last Supper. Jesus had interpreted in advance the meaning of the shedding of his blood the following day and already made it one with the Eucharistic mystery.

By the power of the love with which it was offered in our name, the sacrifice of Christ is all at once the perfect act of adoration, thanksgiving, reparation, and supplication. By means of his Last Supper ritual, Jesus instituted the memorial which would forever make present in the world his one saving sacrifice. The word "memorial" finds its roots in Jewish liturgy, and for the Church it is more than a memory. It is a powerful celebration of God's saving intervention in history, which somehow makes the event present once again. The Lamb of God continues to take away the guilt of the world today through the offering of the Mass. The Mass which we offer daily is a true sacrifice, but it is not a new sacrifice. It is the sacrifice of the Cross; it is the mystical death of Christ.

Since all Old Testament sacrifices prefigured the Cross, all of them were thus oriented towards the Mass which makes it present.[1] Some might object that the Holy Sacrifice of the Mass is not clearly explained in the Bible. The Scriptures are indeed mysterious and must always be interpreted in the light of the ancient tradition of the Church. Yet, with careful meditation of the Bible, it becomes clear that the Eucharist and the sacrifice of the Cross are one mystery. We must understand that the ancient sacrifices, all of which prefigured the Cross, were offered in the Temple. They foreshadowed the Cross and yet they were all cultic or liturgical rituals. The only thing that makes the sacrifice of the Cross into such a ritual is what Jesus said and did in the institution of the Eucharist. Only through the sacrifice of the Mass can ancient biblical worship find its fulfilment in the New Covenant.

Even though all of the Old Testament sacrificial rituals were pointing towards the Mass, the one which teaches us the most about it is that of Passover.[2] Today, the Jewish Passover is merely a commemorative meal, but at the time of Christ it was also a true

1   Saint Thomas Aquinas, *Summa Theologica, Tertia Pars,* Q. 73, Article 6, Main Body.
2   Ibid.

Temple sacrifice.[3] As the Jewish people would sacrifice and then eat their paschal lambs, they somehow believed that this ritual made them one with the initial liberation from Egypt, with the initial paschal lambs of their forefathers. The original exodus was somehow made present to them.[4] They were united to their ancestors across the sands of time by the power of the ritual. Of course, this was only a shadow of what would become a reality when Christ instituted the Eucharistic sacrifice during the course of his last Passover meal. It was a New Passover designed to give all generations the capacity to come into contact with the initial paschal sacrifice of the Lamb of God. During the consecration of the Mass, the priest says that on the night he was betrayed, Jesus took "*this* precious chalice in his holy and venerable hands."[5]

The chalice we raise is truly one with the chalice Christ raised. Just as the paschal lamb once protected the Jewish people from the chastising angel of death, so too, our contact with the Eucharistic Lamb of God shields us from the chastisement merited by our sins, and from that fallen angel whose influence brings eternal death to the soul. Just as the paschal lamb could only be eaten after it had been roasted in the fire, so too we can only consume Christ's glorious flesh once we have first made the fire of his sacrifice present in our own time.

The Catholic teaching on the sacrificial nature of the Mass is not something that was invented by the pious medieval imagination, but rather something which has been there from the very dawn of Christianity. There are many statements of the fathers of the Church which prove that it has always been accepted that the Mass is a true sacrifice.[6] Saint Cyprian summed it up very

3   Brant Pitre, *Jesus and the Last Supper* (Grand Rapids: Eerdmans, 2015) p. 396.
4   Brant Pitre, *Jesus and the Jewish Roots of the Eucharist* (New York: Doubleday, 2011) p.64.
5   Eucharistic Prayer I.
6   See the first chapter of Thomas Crean's book entitled, *The Mass and the*

simply by saying that the sacrifice which we offer is the Passion of the Lord.[1] This doctrine was sadly called into question in a very harmful manner by the attacks made upon the Church by the "reformers" of the sixteenth century. Martin Luther was well aware that the fathers of the Church had taught and accepted the sacrificial nature of the Mass, but so repugnant to him was the idea that anything but faith in Christ could contribute to salvation, that he totally rejected this most ancient of doctrines.

In response to the Protestant attacks, the Council of Trent reaffirmed as a truth to be believed by all Catholics that the Mass is a real sacrifice. The Council proclaimed that through the Mass the bloody sacrifice of Christ is made present in an unbloody mode of offering. Pope Leo XIII would later explain that true religious worship requires sacrifice, and since the only saving sacrifice is that of Calvary, Christ instituted a liturgical rite which would make his sacrifice present throughout history.[2] Speaking of the mystery of Christ's Passion, Pope Pius XII expressed it as follows: "This mystery is the very centre of divine worship since the Mass represents and renews it every day and since all the sacraments are most closely united with the cross."[3]

The Holy Sacrifice and the Saints

Questions have often been asked about how the Cross and the Mass can be said to be one same sacrifice, even though they are offered at completely different moments of human history. When it comes to mystical questions about Calvary and the Mass, we can always turn to the saints in search of light. How is it that many

---

    Saints, (San Francisco: Ignatius Press, 2008).

1   Charles Journet, *The Mass, the Presence of the Sacrifice of the Cross* Translated by Victor Szczurek, (South Bend Indiana: St. Augustine's Press, 2008) p.57.

2   Pope Leo XIII, *Caritatis Studium*, §10.

3   Pope Pius XII, *Mediator Dei*, §164.

of them truly behold and relive the Passion on their beds of pain each Friday? The Crucifixion often seems to be made present to them and even through them. Moreover, why is it that St. Padre Pio would relive the Passion precisely at the moment of the consecration of the Mass? For him the Mass and the Cross were one mystery, and he had the impression that he was hanging upon the Cross rather than standing at the altar when offering the Mass.

If there is no crossover and interaction between the different moments of history, how do we even receive the graces won for us by the Passion today? There must be at least some kind of spiritual interrelation between separate moments of history. How is it that Jesus went so far as to tell Saint Faustina in the 1930's that her love for him had consoled his heart while he was in his agony in the Garden? Even more astonishing, perhaps, was the following statement: "My daughter, My favour rests in your heart. When on Holy Thursday I left Myself in the Blessed Sacrament, you were very much on My mind."[4] The two distinct historical moments of Holy Thursday and a summer's day in 1938 were knit together in the perpetual now of Christ's eternal Person! Other saints have even been convinced that they have witnessed Jesus still sad and grieving with the sorrows of his Passion. Saint Manuel Gonzalez perceived an ocean of bitterness spilling forth from the silence of the tabernacle.

Here are some striking testimonies from the saints about the sacrificial nature of the Mass:

"The Holy Sacrifice is the same as that of the Cross, which was offered once upon Calvary, on Good Friday. The only difference is that when Jesus Christ offered himself on Calvary, the sacrifice was visible; that is to say, Jesus Christ was seen with the bodily eyes, being offered to God, his Father, by the hands of executioners, and shedding his blood, it means that the blood came forth from his veins and was seen flowing down upon the ground. But

4   Saint Faustina, The Diary, §1774.

in the holy Mass, Jesus Christ offers himself to his Father in an invisible and unbloody manner."[1] (Saint Jean-Marie Vianney)

"If we really understood the Mass, we would die of joy. All good works taken together cannot have the value of one Holy Mass, because they are the works of men, whereas the Holy Mass is the work of God."[2] (Saint Jean-Marie Vianney)

"And, therefore, observe that in the Mass there is made not a mere representation, nor a simple commemoration of the Passion and death of the Redeemer, but there is performed, in a certain true sense, the selfsame most holy act which was performed on Calvary."[3] (Saint Leonard of Port Maurice)

"One merits more by devoutly assisting at a Holy Mass than by distributing all of his goods to the poor and travelling all over the world on pilgrimage."[4] (Saint Bernard)

"That same true Lamb, Christ Jesus, who suffered on the Cross, becomes our pasch also on the altar. There are not two paschal victims, not two sacrifices, but one pasch and one sacrifice—one re-presents the other."[5] (Saint John Fisher)

Effects of the Sacrifice

The offering of the Holy Sacrifice brings much grace into the world, whether the priest celebrates alone or with the faithful. In fact, he is never alone, but spiritually united to the entire Church

1 Abbé H. Convert, *The Curé of Ars and the Holy Eucharist* (Minnesota: The Neumann Press, 2000) p.135-136.

2 Thomas Morrow, "The Glory of the Mass", Homiletic and Pastoral Review, July 10, 2014, http://www.hprweb.com/2014/07/the-glory-of-the-mass/

3 Saint Leonard of Port Maurice, The Hidden Treasure: Holy Mass (Charlotte: Tan Books, 2012) p.3.

4 Ibid.

5 Charles Mangan, "Mary and the Eucharist in Saint John Fisher", *Mary at the Foot of the Cross VI* (New Bedford: Academy of the Immaculate, 2007), p.180.

whenever he steps into the sanctuary. The angels themselves accompany him as he processes from the sacristy, for it is both their Lord and his who will soon be present upon the altar of God. Before ever we receive Holy Communion, we are sanctified by our prayerful presence at the Holy Sacrifice of the Mass. The Mass is called a propitiatory sacrifice by the Council of Trent, which means that it appeases the justice of God outraged by our sins. "He was wounded for our transgressions, he was bruised for our iniquities; upon him was the chastisement that made us whole, and with his stripes we are healed" (Isaiah 53:5).

In the extraordinary form of the Mass, the priest prays a beautiful prayer while incensing the altar, asking God to bless the incense as it rises in his presence, and to let his mercy then descend upon us. The Mass is a kind of lightning-rod, deflecting from the corrupt world what it deserves because of its sins. It makes reparation for our past sins and even for the sins of those souls who left this world without being fully prepared for the beatific vision. The universal demands of justice retain those souls in the fires of purgatory, but the merciful gift of the Mass sets them free. How the souls in purgatory now appreciate the sacred hands of the priest. If they could return to the earth, with what reverence would they not participate at the Mass each day! Both the living and the dead receive the benefits flowing out from the glorious sacrifice which transcends all time and space. Since the Mass makes present the mystery of Good Friday, every day is now like the day on which Christ died for the world. His perfect act of "love to the end" is to be found on every altar where Mass is celebrated. Wherever sinners still offend their good God, the Cross is there to make atonement.

A rather poor analogy might help to illustrate the way in which Christ makes reparation for the sins of the nations to the Father through the Mass. The story is told of a popular musician who had wounded the heart of his wife, and who, in order to repair the fault, set about writing her a song to solemnly reaffirm his undying love for her. The song was an instant success, almost immediately topping music charts throughout the world. Now, whenever his wife turned on the radio at home or in the car; even when she would travel to a foreign land, she would inevitably hear her husband's love song, written just for her, being played in airports, shops, and wherever music is to be found. We can imagine the smile returning to her face as she witnessed everywhere the evidence of the sincerity of her husband's love. Sufficient atonement had been made! Similarly, as Christ was instituting the invention of love which we call the Mass, dominant in his mind was the heart of his Father, insulted and offended by the sins of the world. Through the Holy Sacrifice of the Mass, Jesus who has truly become one of us, and who through his Incarnation has personally united every single human soul to himself, offers in our name worthy reparation for our sins. Wherever the Father turns his gaze in this world, he beholds the love of his Son, making up for our lack of love.

Through the liturgy of the Church, in every land and every nation, the sweet plea of Christ's crucified heart rises before the heavenly throne: "Father, forgive them, they know not what they do." Wherever there are sins to be found, the Holy Sacrifice of the Mass is never too far away, so that the Father can always behold the sacrifice of his Son and thus forget about our guilt. Because of the Mass, he can forever look down upon the world with "a serene and kindly countenance."[1] "The world, in fact, since the redemption, is an immense temple where at each moment of time, as the sun advances over a hemisphere, the victim of Calvary is uplifted between heaven and earth by thousands of priests, to the glory of the Most High. Victim essentially immaculate, who keeps his virtue even when he is offered by unworthy hands, Jesus substitutes himself for guilty men, to give to the Father the honour

1   Eucharistic Prayer I

his Sovereign Majesty demands, and to implore his mercy and graces on their behalf."[2]

Through the Mass, the Eucharistic love of the Son counterbalances and outweighs the wickedness of the world. His plea for mercy rings out more powerfully than the angelic demand for justice. Every single day, in thousands of different places, that blood which pleads with more insistence than the innocent blood of Abel is raised before the Face of the Father. The blood of Abel cried out for vengeance; the blood of Christ calls down graces upon those who spilled it. The Mass is the one pure sacrifice which the prophet Malachi said would be offered all over the world polluted by sin. "For from the rising of the sun to its setting my name is great among the nations, and in every place incense is offered to my name, and a pure offering; for my name is great among the nations, says the Lord of hosts" (Malachi 1:11). Only the Mass makes a fulfilment of this prophecy possible, since for the Jewish people sacrifice could only be offered in the temple of Jerusalem. The prophet foresaw the coming of a sacrifice that could be offered in every land.

Without the Mass there would be no hope for the nations submerged in sin, but thanks to the quasi-universal presence of the Mass throughout the world, every day is a new beginning. The guilt of a multitude is blotted out and grace for conversion is offered once again. "For it is only in virtue of the death which Christ suffered that men can satisfy, and that most abundantly, the demands of God's justice, and can obtain the plenteous gifts of His clemency. And Christ has willed that the whole virtue of His death, alike for expiation and impetration, should abide in the Eucharist, which is no mere empty commemoration thereof, but a true and wonderful though bloodless and mystical renewal of it."[3]

2   Abbé H Convert, *The Curé of Ars and the Holy Eucharist* (Minnesota: The Neumann Press, 2000) p.135.
3   Pope Leo XIII, *Mirae Caritatis*, §18.

One of the most important effects of the Mass is that it produces within us the supernatural gift of contrition for our sins. By reverently participating in the Mass, we obtain not only the reparation of our guilt, but also the detestation of our sins. We come to abhor what has wounded the heart of our God. We become like those people who walked away from Calvary beating their breasts (Luke 23:58). Eventually, the Mass will move us towards the disposition of perfect contrition for our sins. Thus, the Holy Sacrifice is an infallible source of salvation, since it is our lack of contrition which separates us from God. The Mass is also an intercessory sacrifice, obtaining God's blessings for the world through the merits of Christ.[1] There are saints who have even managed to raise the dead by the reverent celebration of the Mass for them. Saint Dominic is a case in point.

The Mass is at the same time the perfect sacrifice of thanksgiving (*eucharistesas* in Greek), by means of which we worthily express our gratitude to God for all his blessings. As the priest holds the Eucharistic Lord in his hands and raises him up before the Father, we can simply offer him up in union with the priest, in thanksgiving for all that the good God has done for us. This is a very simple thing to do, and yet it is meritorious, because the love in the heart of Jesus is in itself humanity's most noble act of thanksgiving to God. "Once, St. Teresa of Avila was overwhelmed with God's goodness and asked Jesus, 'How can I thank you?' Our Lord replied, 'Attend one Mass.' More recently, St. Padre Pio said, 'If we only knew how God regards this Sacrifice, we would risk our lives to be present at a single Mass.'[2]

Finally, and perhaps most importantly, the Mass is a sacrifice of adoration, offering to God the kind of gratuitous glorification

---

1   Theologians sometimes refer to this as the power of impetration.
2   Morrow, Thomas. "The Glory of the Mass", Homiletic and Pastoral Review, July 10, 2014, http://www.hprweb.com/2014/07/the-glory-of-the-mass/

which he deserves from his creatures, simply because of who he is. It is the highest act of adoration in the life of the Church. Although, Jesus is God, he is also Man, and as such, his human heart is filled with reverent sentiments of adoration for the Father. Those sentiments are perfectly expressed in the offering of his life to the Father, to which we are united through the Mass. If we ask him, he will offer perfect adoration to the Father in our name. As we join ourselves to the sacrifice of the Mass we should try to hold in our hearts the same dispositions that we know are present in the heart of Jesus, namely, adoration, thanksgiving, reparation, and intercession.

The Mass and Our Sanctification

The priest who offers the Mass is personally sanctified by it, provided that he is well-disposed and offers it with reverence. His personal sanctification is foremost in the order of Eucharistic grace.[3] Although he is in the most privileged position to receive grace from the Mass, he is also in a precarious position, since he is the one most in danger of becoming desensitised to the sacred. A priest must not allow his intimate proximity to the presence of the Lord to undermine his reverence. He must never enter the sanctuary in an unrecollected manner. We should not be surprised that God gives the first fruits of the grace of the Mass to his priest, for there is nothing more fitting than that a priest should be holy. The existence of an unholy priest becomes a kind of perpetual sacrilege.

In his masterly interpretation of the seventeenth chapter of the Gospel of John, Father André Feuillet noticed the parallel between the high-priestly ritual for the Day of Atonement and the high-priestly prayer of Jesus.[4] This chapter of John's Gospel

3   James O'Connor, *The Hidden Manna* (San Francisco: Ignatius Press, 1988) p.302-305.
4   André Feuillet, *Le Sacerdoce du Christ et ses Ministres* (Paris: Téqui, 1971)

which recounts Christ's intercessory prayer as he instituted the Eucharistic sacrifice is divided into three main sections, each of which parallels the three main parts of the ritual of Yom Kippur. Just as the high priest offered sacrifice, first to sanctify the priests of Israel, and only then for the rest of the people of God, so too Jesus prays first for his apostles, to whom he had just given his sacred priesthood, and then for all who would believe in his name. Before he goes to Gethsemane he has already formulated his intention for the distribution of the grace of the Passion. Both then and now, the first fruits of his sacrifice were to be consecrated to the purification of his priests.

In addition to the grace given to the priest, there is a general grace given to the whole Church through the sacrifice of the Mass. We are reminded of the bestowal of this grace by the fact that we must always pray for the Pope, all the clergy and the entire Church, both militant and suffering, at every single sacrificial celebration. By means of it we are also spiritually united to the Church in heaven. As well as this "general" prayer intention for the whole Church, there is also a "particular" intention which the priest presents to God just before he offers the sacrifice. Because he steps into the very heart of the Blessed Trinity at the Mass, the priest has a certain authority in relation to the graces dispensed by the Mass. He is so intimately bound up with the sacrificial mystery, which he offers *in persona Christi* and in the name of the whole Church, that he has the right to direct its flow of grace in some measure towards a particular intention.[1]

Just how much grace is received by the person(s) for whom the Mass is offered will depend upon their own disposition and openness to God. Yet we can be confident that grace will be offered to the one for whom the Mass is offered. A saint would

---

p.22-92.

1   James O'Connor, *The Hidden Manna* (San Francisco: Ignatius Press, 1988) pp. 304-306.

be extremely receptive and inherit choice graces if the Mass were to be offered for him. Saint Faustina was able to feel it immediately when somebody was praying for her before the Blessed Sacrament. She was once awakened by the force of those prayers offered before the Eucharistic Lord during the night.[2] (Adoration during the hours of the night is very powerful. The prayers of those whose love pushes them to sacrifice some of their sleep moves Christ's tender heart.) Saint Faustina's intuition about who was praying for her was confirmed the following day. She could also perceive it when a priest would pray for her and bless her from afar.[3] How much more would she have been affected by a Mass offered especially for her. Other souls, however, are less receptive to the divine activity, but saving graces will at least be offered to them whenever the Mass is celebrated for them.

The amount of grace received depends upon the degree to which the person is spiritually alive, that is, the intensity of his virtues of faith and charity. However, Saint Thomas Aquinas explains that this spiritual life does not necessarily have to be in act, but may simply be in potency. Even if a person is in mortal sin, if his heart is open, then the offering of the Mass can obtain the grace of contrition for him, thereby destroying his mortal sin and bringing his soul back to life in faith and charity.[4] In addition to the particular intention for which the priest offers the Mass, he is obviously also free to present to God whatever personal intention is dear to his own heart in that moment.

The power of the Mass is infinite, but the graces received by the Church at any given time are finite. A certain amount of grace is always given, but the amount of grace depends upon the

2   Saint Faustina, *The Diary*, §1419.

3   Ibid., § 1455.

4   Charles Journet, *The Mass, the Presence of the Sacrifice of the Cross* Translated by Victor Szczurek, (South Bend Indiana: St. Augustine's Press, 2008) p.122.

degree of faith, hope, charity, as well as the spirit of sacrifice in the Church at any given time. It also depends upon the number of souls in the world who are living in the state of deepest union with God, the mystical marriage with Christ. The prayers of these souls unleash grace in torrents, and they personally give the name "Bride of Christ" its deepest possible meaning.[1] Never was there more grace poured out through the offering of the Mass as when the Blessed Virgin Mary still walked the face of the earth. When she could still suffer, offer, and receive Holy Communion with angelic desire, the Church was filled with holy power to convert the world. Her Eucharistic love, joined to the sorrows of her exile here below were strong enough to knock the proud Saul off his horse on the road to Damascus.

Our Lady would have been uniquely receptive to the full force of the grace of the Mass, especially if a Mass had been offered for her and for her intentions.[2] It is not surprising that there exists in the Church to this day the pious practice of priest's being asked to offer Mass for Mary's intentions. She can no longer receive the grace in the way she would have while she was on earth, but she still knows best who is most in need of the grace of the Mass. She daily intercedes for the Church and the world; and if her motherly hands can do much good with the little sacrifices we offer up to God for her intentions, how much more so when we offer up the Holy Sacrifice itself.

The Church's Sacrifice

As well as making Christ's own saving sacrifice present in the world once again, the Mass also joins the sacrifice of the Church to that of her Lord. Christ is a faithful Bridegroom who does

1   Ibid., p.123
2   James O'Connor, *The Hidden Manna* (San Francisco: Ignatius Press, 1988) p. 307.

nothing without his bride.[3] As he advances the redemption of the world through the mystery of the Eucharistic Sacrifice, he does so in union with the Church, joining her offering to his own. During the Offertory of the Mass, as the little drop of water which symbolises humanity is mingled with the wine which symbolises divinity, we are called to mingle our own sacrifices with that of Christ. All that we suffer is given redemptive value and power by being joined to the sacrifice which is just about to be offered to the Father. Our little "deaths" are united to Christ's death through the Mass, and thus they participate in his saving power. Souls can be drawn back to Christ by the gift of our suffering joined to the Passion of the Lord. What we sow in tears can produce eternal joy for others.

The early Church understood this well, and the faithful knew that the passion of the martyrs became one with the Passion of Christ through the daily offering of the Holy Sacrifice. Bystanders declared that at the moment in which the eighty-six year old Saint Polycarp was brutally struck down for his love for Christ, it was made clear to all that he was in some sense becoming "Eucharistic." As his frail old body was hurled upon the fire, the smoke formed the shape of a Church dome above his head, his flesh began to turn white and resemble bread, while all present testified that the sweet aroma of incense filled the air.[4] His death was mystically joined to the sacred liturgy of Christ's Holy Sacrifice. Saint Padre Pio was also given to understand that his sufferings, especially the stigmata which pierced him during the Eucharistic Prayer, were contributing to the salvation of innumerable souls. All souls are saved by Christ alone, but the sufferings of his friends are used by him to bring some of their contemporaries

3   Joaquin Arellano, "The Triple Mediation", *Mary at the Foot of the Cross VI* (New,Bedford: Academy of the Immaculate, 2007) p.45.

4   A Letter on The Martyrdom of Polycarp by the Church of Smyrna, Chapter 15.

back to his one saving sacrifice. This knowledge makes the saints rejoice in suffering; while some of them even go so far as to desire suffering. "Now I rejoice in my sufferings for your sake, and in my flesh I complete what is lacking in Christ's afflictions for the sake of his body, that is, the Church" (Colossians 1:24).

In order for our sacrifices to be acceptable to God at Mass we must be free from grave sin. Saint Paul writes that God chose us in Christ "before the foundation of the world, that we should be holy and blameless before him." (Ephesians 1:4) We have to pause and ponder such a stunning statement. First, he makes the truth of God's all-encompassing eternal gaze perfectly clear, since he knew us and chose us personally before the very foundation of the world. Then he adds that through Christ we are to come into God's presence "holy and unblemished." Here he uses the language of Temple sacrifices, which had to be made holy or set apart for God, and which also had to be without blemish. In the New Testament, there is a transposition of these mysteries. It is not that we must be physically perfect to be united to Christ's sacrifice but we must be morally free from the blemish of serious sin in order to be presented to the Father as an "eternal offering."[1] The sacred character impressed upon our souls in Baptism and Confirmation allows us to participate in the redemptive sacrifice of Christ, joined to the Lord's own offering. This is why the unbaptised would have to leave the Church just before the Eucharistic prayer in ancient times.[2] Just as the sacrificial lambs had to be washed in the pool of Bethzatha before being brought to the Temple, so too, we must be sacramentally washed before we can become living sacrifices through the Mass (John 5:2).

---

1   Eucharistic Prayer III.
2   Charles Journet, *The Mass, the Presence of the Sacrifice of the Cross* Translated by Victor Szczurek, (South Bend Indiana: St. Augustine's Press, 2008) p. 99.

Final Thoughts on the Holy Sacrifice of the Mass

I fear that I may have left the reader with more questions than answers in trying to explain the sacrificial nature of the Mass, but to question is at least a sign that we know we are dealing with something that is beyond us. In the end, perhaps all that our poor minds can fully understand is that the Mass is a great mystery, but it is truly a sacrificial mystery, and this we must profess, even though our understanding cannot ascend to the same heights as our faith. By faith, we approach the consecration as we would the death of Christ. As with all of the transcendent truths of our religion, we can hold to the fact the Mass is a sacrifice with the full assent of our faith, while humbly acknowledging our incapacity to entirely comprehend the doctrine. This is what "mystery" means in the strict sense of the word. Even Saint Padre Pio had to content himself with this much: "What happens in the tremendous time when I am at the altar, I am not able to tell you, because my soul feels it but does not perceive it."[3]

We cannot over-rationalise the truths of our faith in order to fit them all neatly into our categories of understanding. Thus, we should not trouble ourselves too much if our minds cannot exhaust the full divine depths of this mystery. Our hearts at least can perceive something of its grandeur, and this is enough to bring us to our knees in adoration. We must approach the altar of sacrifice with great amazement and external signs of reverence. Kneeling in heartfelt worship is the only appropriate posture for those privileged to be present for the Divine Liturgy. Every physical gesture of kneeling or making a genuflection before the Blessed Sacrament should be accompanied by a deep interior movement of loving adoration. Our inward sentiment must make every outward gesture into an act of profound faith and love for

---

3   Raniero Cantalamessa, *Words of Light: Inspiration from the Letters of Padre Pio* (Massachusetts: Paraclete Press, 2008) p.149

Jesus. The fire in the heart must come out through the body. Pope Benedict XVI explained the indispensable importance of posture, and especially that of kneeling, in his renowned book entitled *The Spirit of the Liturgy*. He makes clear that a liturgy which no longer knows how to kneel before God is one which has forgotten the reason why it exists.

Cardinal Charles Journet describes the folly of those who remain unmoved by the power of the Mass: "They come back from Golgotha and they speak about the weather. If one would tell them that St. John and Mary descended from Calvary speaking of frivolous things, they would say that that's impossible. They, nevertheless, act no differently. (...) There are those who stand for the elevation. I do not know what is of greater wonder, the elevation itself or the attitude of those who see it."[1] Worse still is the attitude of Catholics who want the Holy Sacrifice to be over as quickly as possible, so that they can rush back to their worldly affairs. They have grasped nothing of the magnitude of what is happening before them. All those who come to Mass with anything less than the attitude of reverent adoration come there ill-disposed.

According to Pope Saint John Paul II, there is only so much that we can do when it comes to explaining the fullness of what takes place during the Holy Sacrifice of the Mass: "The Church lives by the Eucharist, by the fullness of this sacrament, the stupendous content and meaning of which have often been expressed in the Church from the most distant times down to our own days. And though this teaching is sustained by the acuteness of theologians, by men and women of deep faith and prayer, and by ascetics and mystics—in complete fidelity to the Eucharistic mystery—it remains incapable of grasping and translating into words what

---

1   Charles Journet, *The Mass, the Presence of the Sacrifice of the Cross* Translated by Victor Szczurek, (South Bend Indiana: St. Augustine's Press, 2008) p. 108.

the Eucharist is in all its fullness, what is expressed by it and what is actuated by it. Indeed, the Eucharist is the ineffable Sacrament!"[2] Only in heaven will we see the truth of the Mass more clearly, and together with the saints, contemplate with wonder all that Jesus has done for us. For now, our darkened minds are blinded by the excess of supernatural light. The one who tries to explain what takes place at the moment of the consecration of the Mass could easily make the statement of Job his own: "I have uttered what I did not understand, things too wonderful for me, which I did not know." (Job 42:3) There is a reason why the priest rises to his feet after offering the mystical death of the Son to the Father and solemnly declares: "*Mysterium Fidei!*" The Mass is the *mystery* of faith *par excellence.*

---

2   Pope John Paul II, *Redemptor Hominis*, §20.

II

A COMMUNION-SACRAMENT

The Manna of Eternity

As the chosen people of Israel journeyed through the desert, on their way to the promised land, the Lord rained down upon them bread from heaven. This mysterious food known as "manna" was to be their sustenance during the time of trial preceding their arrival in the promised land. The parting of the Red Sea waters was merely the debut of their liberation from slavery, an arduous journey still lay ahead of them. Similarly, the saving waters of Baptism are merely the beginning of our passage to eternal salvation. We still have to struggle through the spiritual desert of this world with all of its dangers, if we are to someday arrive at the promised land of heaven. As we set out on this treacherous journey, there is only one nourishment that can keep us alive in the desert: the true Bread from Heaven. Just as God once rained down manna from the skies in the deserted wilderness of Sin, so now he rains down upon our altars each day the real

33

Manna from heaven. If we are to be saved and to have strength to complete the ordeal that has been set before us, we have no other hope but the Eucharist. The daily gift of the manna ceased to fall once the people had safely made it to the promised land, showing us that we are dependent upon the Eucharist until we see the One who hides behind its veil face-to-face in the eternal promised land.

The word manna means "what is this?", and it took its name from the question asked by the children of Israel on the first morning they beheld it on the ground. (Exodus 16:15) Its presence was something of a mystery to them. All that was said of the manna somehow foreshadows what can be said of the Holy Sacrament of the Altar. The Eucharistic Manna is a mystery to us, but then again, all that relates to Christ's body is beyond our understanding. Who can explain how it was conceived, how it was born of the perpetual Virgin Mary, how it was transfigured, or how it appeared at will after the Resurrection? All that relates to the body of Christ can only ever be met with silent awe on the part of poor sinful minds. The manna in the desert had a curious form; it looked more like a white coriander seed than ordinary bread. (Exodus 16:31) We are reminded that a seed is the image that Christ used to describe the Word of God. In spite of its humble appearances, the new Manna of the Eucharist truly contains he who is the Word of God in Person. Thus, it is the seed which implants within us the deepest possible union with the Eternal Word, eventually making us fruitful with every kind of supernatural gift and heavenly blessing. The Eucharistic seed may take time to come to the fruition of holiness, but in a receptive heart it will take effect eventually.

According to Saint Thomas Aquinas, the Eucharist, which makes the Incarnate Word truly present, is the greatest miracle wrought by the Lord (*miraculórum ab ipso factórum máximum.*)[1]

---

1 Saint Thomas Aquinas, *Opusculum* 57, Office for the feast of *Corpus Christi*, 1-4.

In working miracles, God normally intervenes to work some inexplicable visible change in a material reality. In the Eucharist, the wonder worked by the Lord is invisible, escaping the detection of the senses, but it is a wonder nonetheless. We might more properly call the Eucharist the greatest act of Christ's power. Greater than the resurrection of the body of Lazarus is the way in which the dead matter of bread is raised to the supernatural heights of becoming for us the Bread of Life. After the moment of consecration, the substance of bread no longer exists, because it has been changed into the substance of Christ. The Lord is present on the altar in the flesh, so completely present in the fullness of his humanity and divinity, that we call this presence: the Real Presence, in order to distinguish it from the other modes of Christ's presence in the world.

Our senses fail to discern the truth of Christ's presence in the Host and only the baptised soul can perceive it. However, even the baptised soul must work to correct her worldly way of thinking and allow the Holy Spirit to cultivate the gift of ever deeper spiritual vision. If we look at reality in a worldly manner, we will miss the underlying truth of things. When it comes to supernatural realities, the appearances of things can often deceive us. A Roman soldier called Martin once saw a poor man lying at the gates of the city of Amiens, shivering with cold. As he rode past him on his Roman war horse his heart was moved with pity. He returned and cut his long red cloak in two, giving the poor man half of it to warm himself. That night he discovered that the poor man was Jesus Christ and he himself went on to become the great Saint Martin of Tours. Saint Faustina once fed a poor man some warm soup and soon after discovered that the poor man was Jesus Christ. He told her that he had so admired her tender love for the poor that he came down from heaven to experience it for himself.[2] It is said that Saint Alexis who had been away from

2   Saint Faustina, *The Diary*, no. 1312.

his home for many decades returned to his town and spent the rest of his life there as a poor beggar. His family only realised who he was when his body was examined after death, but by then it was too late.[1]

In the spiritual life, the external appearances do not always reveal the truth of the substance to us. This was true in the life of Christ too. Who would have thought that the beautiful young woman walking across the hills of Judea was, in fact, the one who "contained" within her womb the uncontainable Godhead? Who would have thought that the people of Bethlehem were turning away the incarnate God of Israel from their doorstep when they turned away the same young maiden who was about to give birth? Who would have thought that the poor young Carpenter diligently working in the workshop of Nazareth was the glorious Messianic King of Israel? Who would have thought that the Man being mocked by Herod the tetrarch was the true Ruler of the Universe? The Gospel of Luke tells us that Herod and his court treated him with contempt; they literally 'despised' Jesus (Luke 23:11). The word 'despise' implies that they looked down upon him as a person having little or no value. Who would have thought that the poor lonely figure being beaten by the Roman soldiers and judged by Pilate was really the One who will judge the living and the dead? Who would have thought that Simon of Cyrene who was coerced to carry a bloodstained instrument of execution was really carrying the wood that would burst back open the gates of paradise for billions of human souls?

Appearances can be deceptive. Nowhere are the senses more deceived in their perception than when they come into contact with the Eucharist. The Real Presence is out of their reach. In his profoundly theological hymn to the Blessed Sacrament, *Adoro Te Devote*, Saint Thomas Aquinas explains that sight, touch, and

1   Abbé, H. Convert,. *The Curé of Ars and the Holy Eucharist* (Minnesota: The Neumann Press, 2000) p. 23

taste all fail us when it comes to discerning the truth contained in the Eucharist. Hearing alone can come to our aid, for it perceives that Jesus clearly says: "This is my body…" We must ask the Holy Spirit to anoint the faculties of our soul with the gift of deep spiritual vision, so that we can look behind the external veil and glimpse the face of Jesus in the Host that we adore and receive at Mass. To receive him worthily, we must first adore him. The worldly-minded person sees only the external appearances of bread. Like Herod such a person looks down upon the Host, seeing it as something of little or no value. The spiritual person sees that it is really the second Person of the Blessed Trinity. We must pray that we do not end up like the family of Saint Alexis who only realised who he was when they could no longer do anything about it.[2] On the Last Day, Jesus will show us the full stunning reality of what, or rather *who*, was contained in every Host we ever received, but by then it will be too late to change the way we have treated him.

Like the Dewfall

The manna fell upon the desert land each day, mingled with the cool morning dewfall (Numbers 11:6). Saint Thomas Aquinas once taught that this is symbolic for the fact that one of the primary effects of Holy Communion is to cool the heat of our passions and correct that interior disorder of our souls which was introduced by original sin. In fact, the Eucharist is the remedy to the effects of original sin. The communion that was lost with God and neighbour is restored by Holy Communion. Sanctifying grace which unites us to God is deepened, as well as unity with all those who eat the same mystical food as we do. The interior balance of soul over body which was shattered by original sin is also gradually restored by the power of the Blessed Sacrament.

2   *Ibid.*

The holy flesh of Jesus which we take into ourselves each day is the medicine which heals us and puts our flesh back under the direction of intellect and will. "[The Church] believes in the life-giving presence of Christ, the physician of souls and bodies. This presence is particularly active through the sacraments, and in an altogether special way through the Eucharist, the bread that gives eternal life and that St. Paul suggests is connected with bodily health."[1]

We find a good image for the moral healing wrought by Communion in the text in which Jesus enters the house of Peter and heals his mother-in-law. The woman is lying down and unable to move because of an extreme fever (Mark 1:30). The word for fever in Greek comes from the word for fire, and some of the fathers of the Church tell us that this woman is a symbol for the human soul, subject to the domination of the fiery passions.[2] Passions such as lust, anger, hatred, and fear subject the soul to a cruel slavery from which it cannot rise by its own power. As soon as Christ arrives he rebukes the fever and takes the woman by the hand, raising her to her feet. The hand is symbolic for the will, the principle of action, the head is symbolic for the intellect, the principle of thought.

The Real Presence of Christ, entering into our souls, rebukes the passions, cooling their overwhelming power, while raising our will to a supernatural plane, so that it can begin to govern and control them. "Jesus gives the communicant an assured mastery over his passions. In fact, it is the same Jesus Who said, "Have confidence, I have overcome the world," and Who also said to the tempest, "Peace, be still." And now to the proud man, to the miser, to the man who is tormented by the revolt of his senses, to the man who is a slave to his evil inclinations, He says, "Loose

---

1   Catechism of the Catholic Church, §1509.
2   See the summary of the teachings of the Church Fathers contained in the *Catena Aurea* of Saint Thomas Aquinas for an example of such ideas.

him, and let him go." Man finds greater difficulty in correcting or overcoming himself than in performing some exterior good deed, be that deed heroic. Habit is second nature. The Eucharist alone, at least according to the ordinary course of events and of facts based on experience, gives us the power to reform the bad habits that lord it over us."[3]

This is why reverent reception of Holy Communion is said to protect us from future falls into mortal sin. Saint Francis de Sales once provided a curious example in order to explain this effect of Holy Communion. He wrote of a king of ancient times called Mithridates who was so afraid that his mother might be trying to poison him that he developed a strong antidote which he would consume each day. The potent mixture made his body so strong that when he finally decided to take his own life rather than lose his kingdom, he found his body so resistant to the poison he consumed that it had no effect. Similarly, when one receives the Eucharist worthily and well, he becomes so morally strong that the spiritual suicide of mortal sin is less of a threat.[4]

Sweet as Honey

When the Israelites first ate the bread from heaven, they noticed that it tasted like honey (Exodus 16:31). They were prone to losing their faith and trust in God's promises, yielding constantly to discouragement in the desert. The Lord had promised them a land flowing with milk and honey, and so in order to remind them of this promise he sent them this miraculous food as a foretaste of that land. Their feet were still far from the promised land, but already they could almost taste it in the wilderness each day. This is symbolic for the fact that the Eucha-

3   Saint Peter-Julian Eymard, *The Real Presence* (Cleveland: Emmanuel Publishing, 1938) pp. 45-46.
4   Saint Francis de Sales, *Introduction to the Devout Life*, § 20

rist is a foretaste of heaven. Every time we eat the true Manna we are united to the risen glorified flesh of Christ, as a prelude to the resurrection and glorification of our own flesh.

In the Eucharist we taste the sweet delight of the divinity of Christ and already begin to be divinised while still on earth. This divinisation will only be complete in heaven, but through the Host, heaven breaks into time and space. This is why the saints would often undergo their ecstatic experiences during their time of thanksgiving after Mass. Ecstasy is a going out of oneself into God. It brings a taste of what life outside time will be like. The soul granted such favours has already felt something of the ecstatic happiness of eternity. The reason it happens just after Holy Communion is because the Eucharist is a seed of heaven sown upon the earth.

It is important to spend as much time as possible in silent thanksgiving after receiving the Eucharist. The journalist Andre Frossard was touched by the fact that Pope Saint John Paul II would spend about twenty minutes in thanksgiving after Mass, even when people were waiting to have their private audience with him.[1] He ensured that he was faithful to his own private audience with Christ who was really present within him for those fifteen minutes which follow Holy Communion. We should be careful not to lose the precious time in which our poor bodies become tabernacles for the Most High.

Saint Padre Pio shows us the appropriate attitude we should bring to Holy Communion: "The Mass over, I spent time with Jesus to render him thanks. Oh how sweet was the colloquy with Paradise this morning! The heart of Jesus and my heart, excuse the expression, became fused. There were not two hearts that beat, but only one. My own heart disappeared, like a drop of water lost in the ocean. Delightful tears flowed down my face."[2]

1   Andre Frossard, *Be Not Afraid* (New York: St. Martin's Press, 1982) p.32.
2   Fernando Da Riese, *Padre Pio da Pietrelcina: Crocifisso senza Croce* (San

On another occasion he felt that he was almost in paradise: "Yesterday, on the feast of Saint Joseph, only God knows how much sweetness I experienced, especially after the Mass, so much so that I still feel it now. My head and my heart were burning, but with a fire that was doing me good. My mouth experienced all the sweetness of the spotless flesh of the Son of God. Oh, if only in this moment when I still feel almost everything, I could find a way to hold these consolations forever in my heart—I would undoubtedly be in paradise."[3]

We are not all privileged to taste the ecstatic life of heaven every time we receive the Sacred Host, but most of us will experience at least some joy and peace. Those souls who have undergone conversion experiences testify to the fact that once they returned to Holy Mass they began to experience a peace and joy on Sundays that was lacking before. Having returned to the straight and narrow path which leads to the promised land of heaven, they are now permitted to experience a foretaste of heaven's peace and joy in the Eucharist. Saint Jean-Marie Vianney describes for us what he would experience just after receiving Holy Communion: "When we go to Holy Communion, we feel something extraordinary, a well-being which runs through the whole body from head to foot. What is this well-being? It is our Lord, who imparts himself to every part of our body, making it thrill with joy. We are compelled to say like Saint John, *It is the Lord!* Those who feel nothing at all are much to be pitied."[4] Of course we cannot expect to always have sensible consolations at the moment of Communion, but the soul of deep faith will always be aware of the joyful privilege of that moment. The Curé

Giovanni Rotondo: Edizioni Padre Pio, 1975) p.233

3   Raniero Cantalamessa, *Words of Light: Inspiration from the Letters of Padre Pio* (Massachusetts: Paraclete Press, 2008) p.147.

4   Abbé, H. Convert, *The Curé of Ars and the Holy Eucharist* (Minnesota: The Neumann Press, 2000) p. 76.

continues: "When you have had the happiness of receiving the good God, you feel for some time a gladness, a balm in your heart… Pure souls are always like that; and this union is their strength and happiness."[1] If we have not yet tasted the joyful sweetness of the Lord in the Blessed Sacrament, we should turn to Our Lady for help just before we receive it. Saint Bonaventure deems this obligatory: "Anyone who wishes to taste the sweetness of the honey hidden in the Sacrament of the Altar must enjoy the patronage of the Blessed Virgin Mary."[2]

The Hidden Manna and Eternal Life

When Christ himself taught us about the Bread of Life, he insisted upon the fact that it was designed to bring us eternal life. "I am the bread of life. Your fathers ate the manna in the wilderness, and they died. This is the bread which comes down from heaven, that a man may eat of it and not die" (John 6:48-50). The Eucharist is so closely bound up with the bestowal of eternal life that in order to explain this, Jesus used the same solemn sacramental formula he had used when insisting that Baptism is necessary for eternal life. To Nicodemus he had said: "*Truly, truly, I say to you, unless* one is born of water and the Spirit, he cannot enter the kingdom of God" (John 3:5). To those in the synagogue of Capernaum he said: "*Truly, truly, I say to you, unless* you eat the flesh of the Son of man and drink his blood, you have no life in you; he who eats my flesh and drinks my blood has eternal life, and I will raise him up at the last day" (John 6:53-54). "Truly, truly, I say to you, unless…" was Christ's way of insisting on the importance of the truth he was proclaiming. The divine life received

1   Ibid.
2   Mother Maria Francesca Perillo, "Mary Coredemptrix and the Eucharist", *Mary at the Foot of the Cross VI* (New,Bedford:, Academy of the Immaculate, 2007) p. 241.

in Baptism will soon be destroyed by the world, the flesh, and the devil, unless we have constant recourse to the power of the Blessed Sacrament.

There is an interesting statement in the book of Revelation which may help us to look more deeply into the gift of eternal life which is transmitted to us through the Eucharist: "To him who conquers I will give some of the hidden manna, and I will give him a white stone, with a new name written on the stone which no one knows except him who receives it." (Revelation 2:17) The obvious interpretation of the term "hidden manna" would be to see it as some kind of reference to the mystery of the Eucharist. The white stone is more difficult to interpret. There are different ways of doing so, but perhaps one of the more interesting ones is to recall that in the ancient world the white stone with a particular marking upon it was often sent out as an invitation to a great feast.[3] The stone would then provide the guest with access to the event once the occasion had arrived. We are invited to the eternal banquet of heavenly life but in order to access it we must first be given our white stone with a new name written upon it which is personal to us. A new name signifies a new identity.

We all have a unique new identity given to us by the power of Christ's grace. We are called to reflect the face of Jesus in some particular way. Heaven is filled with those souls who did not live by nature alone but who by the power of Christ's grace were recreated in the image of Jesus Christ. In them Jesus reproduced the mysteries of his own life, death, and resurrection. This gift of transformation in Christ is given to us above all through the Hidden Manna of the Eucharist. Our ongoing re-creation in the image of Christ which is itself our entry pass into heaven is deepened each day in Holy Communion.

3   *The Navarre Bible: New Testament* (New York: Scepter Publishers, 2008) p. 987.

Eucharistic Purification

This bread which fell from heaven in the desert was gathered up in such a way that the one who gathered little always had enough and the one who gathered much had not too much. The bread adapted itself to each one in a particular way. Here is what the book of Wisdom says about this mystery: "Instead of these things you gave your people the food of angels, and without their toil you supplied them from heaven with bread ready to eat, providing every pleasure and suited to every taste. For your sustenance manifested your sweetness toward your children; and *the bread, ministering to the desire* of the one who took it, was changed to suit every one's liking" (Wisdom 16:20-21).

What was true naturally in these signs is true supernaturally in the mystery of the Eucharist. Holy Communion "ministers" to the supernatural desire of each person. Those who are 'hungry' will enjoy the Eucharist more than those who have no real supernatural hunger. Those who are starving will be 'filled with good things', as Our Lady taught us in her Magnificat. People enjoy the Real Presence of Jesus according to the degree to which they hunger for God. The spiritually rich are 'sent away empty' from the Eucharistic Banquet, but the spiritually poor have their souls filled (Luke 1:53). In the Gospels it is the humble poor, the sick, and the sinners who find their joy in the presence of Jesus. Saint Mary Magdalene enjoyed nothing but the presence of Jesus after her conversion.

Today some people enjoy nothing more than Eucharistic Adoration and Holy Communion. The spiritually poor are only satisfied by the living presence of God. The simple of heart, those who are unimportant in the eyes of the world, and who are not attached to the apparent greatness of their personalities can be more easily brought to spiritual poverty and the simplicity of love for God alone. These are the kind of people who followed Jesus wherever he went two thousand years ago and who still follow the

Lamb wherever he goes in his Eucharistic state today (Revelation 14:4). An inflated sense of one's own greatness, and the vainglory that goes with it, can be an impediment to hunger for God.

To be hungry in the supernatural order means ceasing to be hungry for worldly things. The more one kind of hunger dies within us, the more a higher hunger comes to life. The Eucharist is the presence of God made flesh, and as such its depths can never be exhausted. No matter how great the hunger, the Eucharist will always be sufficient to satisfy the soul. As Jesus said: "I am the Bread of Life, he who comes to me shall not hunger, he who believes in me shall not thirst" (John 6:35). In fact, there is always more grace in the Eucharist than we can actually contain. The Blessed Sacrament is a never-ending fountain of life-giving grace. From this throne of the Lamb flows the same spiritual river that flows from the 'throne of God' in heaven (Revelation 22:1). Sometimes saints even cease to eat earthly food and live on the Bread from heaven alone, in order to show us just how extraordinary is the mystery contained within it. Since their life had become entirely heavenly, with no trace of worldliness left, their food also became entirely heavenly. Not only does the Eucharist satisfy the longings of the soul but its effects can sometimes even spill over into the body.

When Jesus worked the Eucharistic sign of the multiplication of the loaves of bread, each person ate until he was fully satisfied (John 6:12). The Greek verb for 'satisfy' which John uses, has to do with desire or hunger being completely fulfilled. It could also be translated as 'enjoying', in such a way that implies the fulfilment of one's desires. The Eucharist brings inexhaustible joy to hungry souls because it is a strong foretaste of the heavenly fulfilment of all supernatural desire. The intensity of the foretaste depends upon the desire of the soul. Mary, who teaches us about true spiritual poverty, can put this burning desire for God alone into our souls if we allow her to do so. Aflame with love for the Lord and taking pleasure in him alone, we will come to understand what she meant when she said: "My spirit *rejoices* in God my Saviour." The Eucharistic soul is one that receives the gift of this simple supernatural desire, so that her love might also minister to Christ's desire to be loved. She is called to console the heart of Jesus. How sad it would be for such a soul to turn back to desiring the food of Egypt. The taste for the Bread from heaven is cultivated in a person who leaves the life of Egypt and passes through the desert of detachment.

The time in the desert was a difficult time of purification for the people of Israel. They were still too attached to the things of Egypt and had to be prepared for the great things God had planned for them in the promised land. The manna was given them to keep them alive and to wean them off the food they had been accustomed to while they were slaves. The memory of life in that idolatrous land was being purged away, so that they might be ready to enjoy a new life in Israel. The Eucharistic Manna is provided in order to wean us off the things of this world and to purify us in such a way that we come to desire God alone, and to love all other things in him.

The Eucharist gives us the acquired taste for the Food of the promised land of heaven. Holy Communion and Eucharistic Adoration draw the soul away from earthly attachments. If the Eucharist is not at the centre of our lives, then the purgations of the spiritual life will cause a more bitter form of confusion in the soul. The Eucharistic path of detachment from the world is the most beautiful because the Hidden Manna contains within itself all sweetness. Other paths are more painful. The Eucharist is the clearest testimony to the infinite goodness and patient love of the Lord. If the old manna tasted like honey, it was also to teach us that the true Manna is an invention of the sweet and gentle heart of Christ. Nowhere do we come to encounter the sweetness of his love more powerfully than here.

Eucharistic Negligence

If our hearts are too filled with desires for other things, with inordinate attachments to creatures, there will be no room within them for Jesus. This is one of the problems caused by original sin: we love creatures in an inordinate way and our hearts often have little or no desire for the One for whom they were created. The Eucharistic Lord comes knocking at the door of our hearts but he finds them like the inn of Bethlehem. The soul can go so far as to lose its appetite for the Bread from heaven. One of the greatest sins of the chosen people of Israel in the desert was that they did not appreciate the miraculous gift of the manna. They were not satisfied with it because they had too many desires for other things which they had known in Egypt. We notice that the greatest chastisement that came upon the people of Israel in the desert, came just after they had said that they "loathed" the "worthless food" of the manna from heaven (Numbers 21:5). This extreme ingratitude manifested their lack of trust in God's goodness. They had blasphemously accused him of bringing them out into the wilderness just to watch them die, and so they show that they had lost their faith in the promise of a land flowing with milk and honey. This was followed by the arrival of fiery serpents which brought death to many among them. The word "fiery" refers perhaps to the terrible burning sensation that followed upon the snakebite.

The people had rejected and spurned the gift which was a manifestation of God's providential love. How much more serious would it be to reject or spurn the true Manna of the Eucharist, which is not just a sign of God's providential love, but the very incarnation of that love. Saint Faustina once felt that she heard Christ say that Catholics who spurn his love in Holy Communion wound his heart most bitterly. The only image that might give us some idea of the pain they cause him would be to picture a most loving mother who is rejected by her own children:

Oh, how painful it is to Me that souls so seldom unite them-selves to Me in Holy Communion. I wait for souls, and they are indifferent toward Me. I love them tenderly and sincerely, and they distrust Me. I want to lavish My graces on them, and they do not want to accept them. They treat Me as a dead object, whereas My Heart is full of love and mercy. In order that you may know at least some of My pain, imagine the most tender of mothers who has great love for her children, while those children spurn her love. Consider her pain. No one is in a position to console her. This is but a feeble image and likeness of My love.[1]

Sins of irreverence, sacrilege, or indifference to the Eucharist are among the most serious we can commit in the desert of this world. The Vulgate Bible tells us that the people in the desert complained that the manna was "light food" (Numbers 21:5). It did not appear to be substantial enough for their worldly cravings. This represents the complaint of one who loses his faith in the Real Presence of Christ. Failing to perceive the substantial presence of the God-Man in the Host, the worldly person's gaze only perceives the appearances, and thus concludes that the Blessed Sacrament is light food indeed; while in reality, the Eucharist is the heavenly food which gently falls upon our altars, the miraculous healing manna, which cools the heat of our passions like the dewfall. Once we reject it, the evil serpents will have their way in our lives.

Those who reject the Eucharist and who lose their taste for the things of God are in serious danger of falling in the desert of this world. Our safe journey to the promised land depends upon how well we live from the grace that is available to us in the Blessed Sacrament. It contains all that we need in order to remain spiritually strong and healthy. We must learn to be satisfied with

1   Saint Faustina, *The Diary*, §1447.

the Eucharist alone, for as humble as it may appear, it is the real and living presence of the One who is the joy of heaven and earth, the One who satisfies the angels and saints in paradise. The Curé of Ars had the right attitude towards this gift: "O sweet banquet, heavenly bread! Ah, what a privilege to be able to feed our souls, and to feed them on God!"[2] Truly we can say with the Psalmist: "Men ate the bread of angels, he sent them provisions in abundance" (Psalm 78:25).

Eucharistic Virtues

As well as detaching us from sin and worldliness, the Eucharist sanctifies us. It both purifies and elevates the faculties of the soul, feeding the life of Christ within us. To the well-disposed heart it brings an infusion of Christ's own holiness. If we are already receiving it regularly without growing in holiness, then there must be some obstacle to grace in our hearts. It may be that we have an affection for some sin, even a venial sin, which we must seek to purify immediately. A lukewarm attitude in relation to overcoming sinful tendencies is often the cause of spiritual stagnation. Unforgiveness, unholy desires, and ill-will towards others, are also particularly common obstacles to spiritual growth. Or, it may be that we have to increase the intensity of the faith and desire with which we approach the Sacrament of Love.

Saint Catherine of Genoa felt as though she could die from the sheer intensity of the desire that gripped her loving heart when she would see the Host in the priest's hands. If we are not aflame with love when we receive the Lord then we approach him ill-disposed. A sufficient time spent in preparation for Mass helps us to stoke up the fire of our desire, so that we can welcome the Lord in a warm and fitting manner when he comes "under

2   Abbé, H. Convert, *The Curé of Ars and the Holy Eucharist* (Minnesota: The Neumann Press, 2000) p. 50.

our roof." Saint Francis de Sales recommends that we begin our preparation the evening before we are to receive the Lord: "Begin your preparation over-night, by sundry aspirations and loving ejaculations. Go to bed somewhat earlier than usual, so that you may get up earlier the next morning; and if you should wake during the night, fill your heart and lips at once with sacred words wherewith to make your soul ready to receive the Bridegroom, who watches while you sleep, and Who intends to give you countless gifts and graces, if you on your part are prepared to accept them."[1]

PURITY

If we prepare and purify our hearts to receive the Lord, while also taking the time to silently give him thanks after Holy Communion, then we will be raised to new heights of holiness. Some saints were totally transformed on the day of their very first Holy Communion. Saint Catherine Labouré was "unrecognisable" after that first encounter with the Eucharistic Lord. Her sister said that she became "all mystical."[2] Saint Jean-Marie Vianney was looked upon as a little saint from that day forward.[3] Saint Therese of Lisieux said that she herself disappeared in that moment and Jesus took control of her life.[4] For those of us who are not as pure or well-disposed as they were, the transformation is more gradual. The story is told of a person who once went to a saintly priest and said: "Father, I have been going to daily Communion for years, but I am still lazy, impatient, glutton-

---

1   Saint Francis de Sales, *Introduction to the Devout Life*, 2:21.

2   These details were provided by Father Michel-Marie Zanotti in his homily entitled: "*La Vie de Sainte Catherine Labouré*" given in the Church of Saint Vincent de Paul, Marseille, France, November 27th 2011.

3   Abbé, H. Convert, *The Curé of Ars and the Holy Eucharist* (Minnesota: The Neumann Press, 2000) p. 60.

4   Saint Therese of Lisieux. *The Story of a Soul*. Translated by John Beevers, (New York: Doubleday, 1989) p. 53.

ous, proud, vain…" The priest interrupted the woman with the reply: "Can you imagine what you would be like without daily Communion?"

We may not always be aware of the flowering of Christian virtues in our souls, but through Communion Jesus is certainly active within us, preserving us from moral disintegration and gently leading us to sanctity. We are reminded of the words of Saint Francis de Sales: "The most fragile, easily spoilt fruits, such as cherries, apricots, and strawberries, can be kept all the year by being preserved in sugar or honey; so what wonder if our hearts, frail and weak as they are, are kept from the corruption of sin when they are preserved in the sweetness ("sweeter than honey and the honeycomb") of the Incorruptible Body and Blood of the Son of God."[5] The saint said something similar in speaking of the virtue of purity: "While fruits are whole, you may store them up securely, some in straw, some in sand or amid their own foliage, but once bruised there is no means of preserving them save with sugar or honey. Even so, the purity which has never been tampered with may well be preserved to the end, but once that has ceased to exist nothing can ensure its existence but the genuine devotion, which, as I have often said, is the very honey and sugar of the mind."[6]

Once we have damaged any particular virtue, especially that of purity, it can still be restored and preserved, but only if we immerse ourselves often in the sweetness of love emanating from the Eucharistic Heart of Jesus. It would be gravely sacrilegious to receive the Eucharist with anything less than a pure heart. If we have freely and deliberately consented to unchaste desires or acts, then we may not receive Communion until we have first been to Confession. An act of contrition is insufficient.[7]

5   Saint Francis de Sales, *Introduction to the Devout Life*, 2:20.

6   Ibid. 3:12

7   James O'Connor, *The Hidden Manna* (San Francisco: Ignatius Press,

The Catechism reminds us that true purity of heart requires three things: chastity, orthodoxy, and charity.[1] Purity is not simply a question of being chaste in body and desire by observing the sixth and ninth commandments. If we sin against the true and orthodox Catholic faith by consenting to doubts or accepting erroneous theological principles, we have lost our purity of soul. We must repent immediately. Similarly, if we hold hatred for others in our thoughts or in the movements of our hearts, then we are no longer pure before God. In order to have these three dimensions of purity of heart, we need to have recourse to three other realities. The French call these three realities *"les trois blancheurs"*, the three things that keep us in the bright white light of holy purity. The word *"blancheur"* means "whiteness." These three realities are: love for the white Eucharistic Host, devotion to the Immaculate Heart of Mary, the one whose soul is whiter than snow, and full communion with the Holy Father dressed in white. If we deliberately separate ourselves from the pope in our hearts or by our actions, then we will soon lose the bright purity of soul that comes to us through communion with the holy Catholic Church. We must be in full communion with the pope, and the bishop he sends us, in order to benefit from Holy Communion.

Communion with the mystical body of Christ is necessary in order to be able to have communion with his living Eucharistic body. Pope Pius XI explains for us the nature of true communion in the Catholic Church: "He wanted the apostles as a body to be intimately bound together, first by the inner tie of the same faith and love which flows into our hearts through the Holy Spirit, and, second, by the external tie of authority exercised by one apostle over the others. For this he assigned the primacy to Peter, the source and visible basis of their unity for all time."[2] To say that

---

1988) p. 224.

1   Catechism of the Catholic Church, §2518.

2   Pope Pius XI *Ecclesiam Dei*

communion with the pope is the external tie which binds us together does not mean that it only relates to external structures. It has a real spiritual power. It is akin to a sacramental sign which makes present a reality. If we deliberately reject the external tie, we soon lose the internal tie which it represents.

Without the external apostolic bond of communion, our unity with others in the Church—which is the intended effect of Holy Communion—will soon disintegrate. True supernatural unity among Catholics is the work of the Holy Spirit, but he uses the visible instrument of the papacy to safeguard it. The Holy Spirit is given only to the obedient (Acts 5:32). If we are united to Our Lady and the Pope, receiving Holy Communion with purity of heart, then it will be a most fruitful experience. Our souls will come to shine ever more brightly with Christ's own purity. We can conclude with one final image from Saint Francis de Sales which he uses in order to describe the virtue of Eucharistic purity. The saint had often watched the beautiful little hares running across the Alpine mountains and noticed that some of them turned white in winter. Not knowing the scientific reasons for this change of colour, he conjectured that it took place because the hares had nothing to eat in winter except snow. Similarly, the soul who feasts often on the purest body of Christ soon "turns bright" with his own immaculate purity.[3]

HUMILITY

Purity and all of the other virtues are strengthened by contact with the holy body of Christ, but there are some particular virtues which shine more brightly in deeply Eucharistic souls. Chief among them is the virtue of humility. This is the all-important virtue which constitutes the only solid foundation upon which the edifice of holiness can be built. Spiritual writers often list the three most important virtues as: "humility, humility, and humil-

3   Saint Francis de Sales, *Introduction to the Devout Life*, §21.

ity." The Eucharist is the source of all true supernatural humility because in it Christ continues to display this virtue to a heroic degree. In his *Adoro Te Devote*, Saint Thomas Aquinas tells us that in the humiliation of the Crucifixion Jesus hid his divinity, but in the Host he hides his very humanity. In his unfathomable humility, he who is the source and summit of all glory, beauty and power remains forever hidden behind the fragile white Eucharistic veil. Those who are deeply devoted to him in his Eucharistic state come to reflect this noble virtue.

Saint Jean-Marie Vianney is a prime example of this virtue because he was such a deeply Eucharistic soul. His brother priests once organised a petition against him which was to be signed by as many pastors as possible in the diocese and then sent to the bishop. Somehow, the petition also arrived in the parish of Ars. When the saint read the letter in which his brother priests said that he was not intelligent enough to be a pastor, rather than break down in sadness or fly into a proud rage, he signed it too![1] Upon seeing his signature, the bishop recognised that they had a true saint in their midst. This kind of sublime humility which shines most brightly in the saints of the Catholic Church comes from frequent contact with the Eucharistic Lord.

FORTITUDE

The virtue of fortitude is also renewed and strengthened through the gift of Holy Communion. When Elijah had lost his courage because of the infidelity of his people, and collapsed in self-pity, he was given a mysterious bread which so fortified his body that he could walk for forty days by its power (1 Kings 19:8). The Eucharist is that heavenly Bread which strengthens the soul and raises it up from discouragement, permitting it to continue to walk with ever-growing strength along the path of salvation.

1 Goerge Rutler, *The Curé d'Ars Today* (San Francisco: Ignatius Press, 1998) p.185.

When Saint Jean-Marie Vianney would be tempted to yield to discouragement because of all of the attacks he sustained and the calumnies that were circulating about him, he would always return to his mission with great strength after receiving Holy Communion. He would be like a man reborn. So striking was the difference in his demeanour before and after Communion, that somebody asked him what had happened and he responded that he had just been bathed in love.[2] Contact with infinite divine love renews and strengthens the soul. Here is how Saint Faustina described the strength she would draw from Communion and adoration, around which her entire life revolved: "I find myself so weak that were it not for Holy Communion I would fall continually. Jesus concealed in the Host is everything to me. From the tabernacle I draw strength, power, courage and light. Here, I seek consolation in time of anguish. I would not know how to give glory to God if I did not have the Eucharist in my heart."[3]

FAITH, HOPE, AND LOVE

Above all it is the theological virtues of faith, hope, and love which are strengthened by the power of the Blessed Sacrament. Every time we adore the Host and receive it worthily, these virtues are fortified within us. The Eucharist is the hardest of all the mysteries to comprehend, and so true faith in it is very meritorious. In some sense it is the crown of faith. Every time we look at the Host and say "I believe" we automatically renew our faith in all of the other mysteries of Christ. If he is there in the Host, then that means he is the Son of God who alone has the power to do such a thing. If he is the Son of God, then we also profess his Incarnation, which itself was the fruit of the Holy Spirit in the womb of the Virgin Mary. If we believe Christ is truly

2   Abbé, H. Convert, *The Curé of Ars and the Holy Eucharist* (Minnesota: The Neumann Press, 2000) p. 80.
3   Saint Faustina, *The Diary*, §1037.

the Son of God, then we also profess our faith in his Father, and all that Christ has revealed to us about him. Every act of faith in the Eucharist is *ipso facto* an act of faith in the entire deposit of divine revelation.

Holy Communion also deepens the theological virtue of hope. Supernatural hope relates to the goodness of the God who loves us enough to prepare a place for us in the happiness of his eternity. The Eucharist is the manifestation of that loving goodness as well as a foretaste of eternal happiness. Every time we look at the Host, all doubts about God's goodness are removed. How could we doubt the love of a God who becomes a Child, who dies for us, and who then goes so far as remaining with us forever behind the humble appearances of bread? His love to the extreme is revealed in the Cross and in the Eucharist.

As well as nourishing our hope by revealing God's love to us, the Eucharist also nourishes and strengthens our capacity to love. Saint Therese of Lisieux noticed that early on in his public ministry, Jesus had said: "love your neighbour as yourself", but on the night he instituted the Eucharist he said: "love one another as I have loved you" (John 13:34). The difference is immense. Through the Eucharist we come to perfect love, to the imitation of his own "love to the end" because he himself loves through us. He puts into our hearts of stone his own heart of flesh and raises our poor hearts to a new degree of charity. The precious blood of Jesus in the chalice retains the appearances of wine to show us that it is by means of his Real Presence that Christ makes us branches of the vine and that the sap of his own love now runs through us.[1]

As though to make us understand that the Blessed Sacrament is a mystery of love, when Jesus reveals his Real Presence through a Eucharistic miracle, it is often heart tissue that the scientists detect when examining the Host. In one of the most

---

1   Gaudentius of Brescia, Office of Readings, Thursday, Week 5 of Eastertide.

recent cases which took place in Buenos Aires in the 1990's the scientists confirmed that the sample of the Host they analysed was indeed human flesh taken from that part of the heart which pumps the blood around the body.[2] Holy Communion is an encounter with the entire Person of Christ, body, blood, soul, and divinity, but he reveals his heart to us in the Eucharistic miracles in order to remind us that it is all of his love that he pours into us in that moment.

It is in receiving Holy Communion, that we experience the truth of the astonishing words he spoke at the Last Supper: "As the Father has loved me, so have I loved you" (John 15:9). We are loved with a love which reflects the infinite, perfect, divine love of the Eternal Father for the Son. The only fitting response to that gift is to return him love for love. The Eucharist is the Sacrament of Divine Love and through Holy Communion we come to love with an eternal kind of love. The Eucharist is the secret of the saints and the reason why they come to be able to give of themselves unceasingly. In the life of the saints, we glimpse something of the life of Christ who gave every last drop of his blood out of love for souls and who now continues to give his heart fully to all who approach him in Holy Communion. "While it nourishes us with Christ, the Eucharist which we celebrate transforms us little by little into the body of Christ and spiritual food for our brothers and sisters."[3]

Holy Communion and the Other Sacraments

Pope Leo XIII was convinced that the entire life of the Church is sustained by the power of the Eucharist and oriented towards its glorification. Even the other six sacraments are all ordered to the Eucharist. "This Sacrament, whether as the theme of devout medi-

2   Piotrowski, Mieczyslaw, "Eucharistic Miracle in Buenos Aires", (Love One Another: E-Journal 12/14/2010)
3   Pope Francis, General Audience, August 17, 2016.

tation, or as the object of public adoration, or best of all as a food to be received in the utmost purity of conscience, is to be regarded as the centre towards which the spiritual life of a Christian in all its ambit gravitates; for all other forms of devotion, whatsoever they may be, lead up to it, and in it find their point of rest."[1] The Eucharist is the super-sacrament, the sacrament towards which all the others tend, and out of which their power flows.[2]

Although Christ has willed that each sacrament should have its own unique function, all that the other sacraments accomplish derives its power from the Eucharist. Each of the other sacraments then prepares us to return to the Eucharist and draw graces from it ever more abundantly. This mutual sacramental enrichment is true above all in relation to the sacrament of Confession. Confession and the Eucharist always go hand in hand. We cannot encounter Christ in a personal way until we have first repented of our sins. This is why Saint John the Baptist came with his message of repentance before the arrival of Christ. Our first Holy Communion is always preceded by our first Confession to ensure that we will always know our need to return to God's friendship before we receive his Real Presence. The more time we spend in adoration and the more worthily we receive Communion, the more our consciences are enlightened, permitting us to make ever more humble and contrite confession of our sins. The two sacraments thus make each other more fruitful.

The intrinsic connection between the two sacraments is illustrated in the lives of Christians of every generation. The life of Blessed Charles de Foucauld offers us a shining example. In his youth he had lived a most sinful and wretched existence. Having lost his faith in his teenage years, he handed himself over to a life of debauchery for over a decade. Sick of the emptiness of his pitiable

---

1   Pope Leo XIII, *Mirae Caritatis*, § 14.
2   James O'Connor, *The Hidden Manna* (San Francisco: Ignatius Press, 1988) p. 314-315, 323.

existence, he eventually began to search for religious meaning once again. After years of aimless wandering, he returned to Paris at the age of twenty-eight and sought out an intelligent priest with whom he might discuss the doctrines of the faith in depth. A renowned man of God called Father Huvelin was at that time stationed in the Church of Saint Augustin in Paris. Charles made his way there one morning and came upon the priest in his confessional.

After having tried to initiate some kind of purely intellectual dialogue, Charles found himself faced with a moment of grace; the moment of grace upon which all other graces in his life would depend. The holy priest was not interested in intellectual debates but in the salvation of the soul of this lost sheep. His biographer, Jean-Jacques Antier, describes how the conversation went on that fateful morning of grace:

> Charles leaned toward him and, without kneeling, murmured in a voice overcome by emotion: 'Father, do not be surprised. I do not come for Confession. I do not have the faith. I only wish to learn some things about the Catholic religion.'
>
> Father Huvelin fixed his eyes on him: 'You do not have the faith? Have you never believed then?'
>
> 'Yes, thirteen years ago. But right now, I am unable to believe. There are all the obstacles of the mysteries, the dogma, the miracles.'
>
> 'You are mistaken, my son. What is missing now, in order for you to believe, is a pure heart. Go down on your knees, make your confession to God, and you will believe.'
>
> 'But, I have not come for that!'
>
> 'That does not matter. Go down on your knees and say the *Confiteor*.'[3]

3   Jean-Jacques Antier, *Charles de Foucauld*. Translated by Julia Shirek Smith, (San Francisco: Ignatius Press, 1999) p.100

Charles reluctantly obeyed and after a long, sincere confession of all the evil he had committed, the moment of absolution arrived. His soul was filled with an incomprehensible joy and peace. All the obstacles to faith which he thought that he had vanished in an instant. Sin was the only obstacle blocking the Holy Spirit from entering his heart. Not only did he believe, he knew![1] His step was light, as the priest commanded him to go straight to the altar rails and receive Holy Communion.

The wise pastor of souls who understood the link between the sacrament of Confession and the sacrament of the Eucharist, knew that he must immediately send Charles to receive Holy Communion to complete the grace of that morning. The act of reconciliation was merely the preparatory grace for encountering the Person of Christ in the flesh. In that instant of his first worthy Communion Charles de Foucauld was transformed forever. He said that on that morning of grace he became a child all over again. The peace, the joy, the purity of childhood came back to his heart in a flood. He would live for Jesus alone from that day onwards. He went on to become a Eucharistic hermit, spending hours and hours before the Blessed Sacrament each day. In one of his letters, he speaks of spending fifteen hours in one day in Eucharistic Adoration.[2] The life of Eucharistic love which would become his vocation was the fruit of that moment in which he first confessed his sins and approached the Bread of Life. If we receive Holy Communion in a state of grace, after having sincerely confessed all of our sins, then the Eucharist will rapidly transform our souls.

On the other hand, to receive the Eucharist with the stain of original sin or unconfessed mortal sin upon our souls would be a grave betrayal of the Lord. The teaching authority of the Church as expressed through the word of her preachers constitutes the

1 *Ibid* p. 101.
2 See http://www.adoperp.fr/index.php/bx-charles-de-foucauld.html

flaming sword which must still protect the Tree of Life from profanation by those who have not yet been washed from their sins by the power of Christ's merits (Genesis 3:24). Examining oneself, having sincerely done everything possible to be in a state of grace, is always the necessary preparation for Holy Communion. Those who receive unworthily are guilty of having shed the blood of Christ (1 Corinthians 11:27). The term employed by Saint Paul to describe this sin is surprisingly strong.

In spite of the crystal-clear teaching of the Church, there will always be souls who approach the Lord unworthily, as well as pastors who condone their sacrilege. There are also pastors and teachers who even go so far as to deny the Real Presence of Christ in the Eucharist, both by their words and their manner of celebrating the sacred mysteries. This is nothing new. "Every account of the Eucharist given in the New Testament contains the theme of betrayal: the sixth chapter of John, the Synoptic accounts of the Institution with their references to Judas' deed; the words of Paul in 1 Corinthians 11 about those who eat and drink unworthily. The Sacrament of his Presence continues the Mystery of his Person: a sign of contradiction."[3] Also, we cannot but notice that the consecration of the Eucharist is preceded by a reference to the treachery of Judas. (See Eucharistic Prayer III for example.) The Blessed Sacrament is the presence of Eternal Love who makes himself vulnerable for love of us. Vulnerability is always in danger of being exploited by the wicked. There is something analogous between the state of the infant Jesus in Bethlehem and his state in the Eucharist. There, he was helpless and completely at the mercy of the love of Mary and Joseph. In the sacred species of the Eucharist, he has entrusted himself to us, putting himself entirely at the mercy of our love.

3   James O'Connor, *The Hidden Manna.* (San Francisco: Ignatius Press, 1988) p. 163.

Eucharistic Transformation

In his different writings and homilies, Pope Benedict XVI spoke often of the power of the Eucharist to transform and divinise our souls. In his homily to the young people at World Youth Day in 2005, the Pope enunciated a profound idea, which he would take up again a couple of years later in the document entitled *Sacramentum Caritatis.* The mystery of the Eucharist is above all a mystery of transformation. The Eucharist makes present the sacrifice of Calvary, in which hatred was absorbed by the heart of Jesus and transformed into love, in which death was transformed into life, and sin into sanctifying grace. On the Cross Jesus uses the cruel violence that is being inflicted upon him as the means of immolating his life in love. This sacrifice he offers even for the very people who are torturing him. The outpouring of hatred is simultaneously being overcome by an even greater outpouring of love. His interior attitude completely changes the nature of what is happening.

The book of Exodus offers us a type of the transformative power of Christ's sacrifice. When the chosen people of Israel first came into the wilderness, having just crossed the Red Sea, they went in search of drinking water. After three days they drew near to the River Marah but were unable to drink its waters because they were bitter. Moses then hurled a tree into the river and the waters suddenly became sweet and drinkable (Exodus 15:25). Jesus, the true liberator, hurled the wood of the Cross into the torrent of suffering which we call human history. By the power of his Cross, the value of suffering was transformed and the sorrow of all those who are united to Christ was sweetened. Now our sufferings produce spiritual life and eternal glory. By means of the Mass, the power of the Cross constantly mingles with the sorrow of human history making all that we must suffer sweet and life-giving. So, the first dimension of transformation which we encounter in the Eucharist relates to the fact that it makes present the sacrifice of Calvary, the mystery through which sorrow has been made bearable.

In the sacrament of the Eucharist there is also the transformation whereby the bread becomes the living body of Christ and the wine becomes his precious blood. Both the sacrificial transformation and the sacramental transformation are designed to bring about the transformation of our souls. Through participation in the sacrifice of the Mass and Holy Communion our hearts are gradually changed and we become the saints we are called to be. This Eucharistic transformation which we can already observe taking place in individual souls will ultimately lead to the complete transformation of the universe at the end of time. However, all of the divine power which transforms our souls, and ultimately the world, is already contained in the Eucharist. In fact, it was already contained in the first consecration of the Eucharist by Jesus Christ in the Cenacle. The divine glory and power contained in the little white Host are nothing less than the glory and power which will one day be manifest for all the world to see, but for now faith alone can pierce this mystery. This is how the pope explains the extraordinary chain of Eucharistic transformations:

> By making the bread into his Body and the wine into his Blood, (Jesus) anticipates his death, he accepts it in his heart, and he transforms it into an action of love. What on the outside is simply brutal violence—the Crucifixion— from within becomes an act of total self-giving love. This is the substantial transformation which was accomplished at the Last Supper and was destined to set in motion a series of transformations leading ultimately to the transformation of the world when God will be all in all (cf. 1 Cor 15: 28). In their hearts, people always and everywhere have somehow

expected a change, a transformation of the world. Here now is the central act of transformation that alone can truly renew the world: violence is transformed into love, and death into life. Since this act transmutes death into love, death as such is already conquered from within, the Resurrection is already present in it. Death is, so to speak, mortally wounded, so that it can no longer have the last word.[1]

The pope then went on to explain the power of the Eucharist by way of an interesting analogy taken from the world of science:

To use an image well known to us today, this is like inducing nuclear fission in the very heart of being—the victory of love over hatred, the victory of love over death. Only this intimate explosion of good conquering evil can then trigger off the series of transformations that little by little will change the world. All other changes remain superficial and cannot save. For this reason we speak of redemption: what had to happen at the most intimate level has indeed happened and we can enter into its dynamic. This first fundamental transformation of violence into love, of death into life, brings other changes in its wake. Bread and wine become his Body and Blood. But it must not stop there; on the contrary, the process of transformation must now gather momentum. The Body and Blood of Christ are given to us so that we ourselves will be transformed in our turn. We are to become the Body of Christ, his own Flesh and Blood.[2]

We are called to let ourselves be interiorly transformed and then this transformation is called to pass out through us and end in the transformation of the world. The Eucharist already contains the transforming power which will ultimately lead to

1 Pope Benedict XVI, *Homily for World Youth Day* 2005.
2 Pope Benedict XVI, *Homily for World Youth Day* 2005.

the transformation of the entire universe at the end of time. The heavenly power is already at work, but not yet fully unleashed. The analogy with nuclear physics is worthy of consideration. Nuclear fission is a process which was discovered in the 1930's whereby the nucleus of an atom is split and multiplies, leading to a release of great energy which has been harnessed so as to produce nuclear power. The splitting of the atom can be channelled in such a way as to cause a nuclear chain reaction and ultimately a powerful explosion. By this analogy the Pope wanted to make us understand the extraordinary spiritual energy contained in every single consecrated Host; so that we might allow ourselves to be drawn into the chain reaction of transformations that will ultimately culminate in an explosion of love sufficient to transfigure the entire universe on the Last Day. It is as though the "Divine Scientist" split the atom at the moment of the institution of the Eucharist, and someday the atomic bomb of transforming love will explode and all things will be made new.

Final Thoughts on Holy Communion

The Eucharist is the Bread from heaven, allowing us to glimpse and taste the joy of paradise while still on earth. The Council of Trent made this heartfelt plea to the children of the Church, that they might stay faithful to the great mystery of the Eucharist:

And finally this holy Synod with true fatherly affection admonishes, exhorts, begs, and beseeches, through the bowels of the mercy of our God, that all and each of those who bear the Christian name would now at length agree and be of one mind in this sign of unity, in this bond of charity, in this symbol of concord; and that mindful of the so great majesty, and the so exceeding love of our Lord Jesus Christ, who gave His own beloved soul as the price of our salvation, and gave us His own flesh to eat, they would believe and venerate these sacred mysteries of His body and blood with such constancy and firmness of faith, with such devotion of soul, with such piety and worship as to be able frequently to receive that supersubstantial bread, and that it may be to them truly the life of the soul, and the perpetual health of their mind; that being invigorated by the strength thereof, they may, after the journeying of this miserable pilgrimage, be able to arrive at their heavenly country, there to eat, without any veil, that same bread of angels which they now eat under the sacred veils.[1]

The Council's use of the term "supersubstantial" bread is a reference to the petition for daily bread which we make in the Our Father. The literal word used by Christ in the Gospel is "supersubstantial" (*epiousios*) and it could even be translated as "supernatural."[2] We might make a daily morning petition to our Heavenly Father in this way: "Give us this day our Supernatural Bread of the Eucharist!" The Church allows multiple levels of interpretation of these words of the Lord's Prayer, but truly the Eucharist is a supernatural reality which she implores us to treat as our greatest treasure and love.

In the wondrous Host, and in the lives of those who are transformed by its power, we catch a glimpse of the world to come, of the civilisation of perfect love. Holy Communion is the necessary sustenance of the Church's life and without it the holiness of her children would be no more. We can never be grateful enough for the gift of Holy Communion. Those souls who could easily make it to Mass on a regular basis but who choose to spend all of their time on other things are greatly to be pitied. The saints, who are most fully endowed with gifts of spiritual sensitivity and

---

1   Council of Trent, Thirteenth Session, Chapter VIII.
2   Brant Pitre, *Jesus and the Last Supper,*. (Grand Rapids: Eerdmans Publishing, 2015) p. 172.

discernment, instinctively perceive that Holy Communion is the only source of true happiness on earth. They approach it with seraphic desire, purifying their hearts, and spending much time in preparation for Mass, as well as much time in thanksgiving afterwards. They live from one Holy Communion to the next. If we imitate them in this simple way of life, we too will become holy and taste the life of heaven while still on earth. The famous phrase of Saint Jean-Marie Vianney offers us the perfect conclusion to these thoughts on Holy Communion: "There is nothing so great as the Eucharist. If God had something more precious, he would have given it to us!"

III

A PRESENCE-SACRAMENT

The Exile from Eden

Man was made to live in intimacy with God. Human nature was never intended to exist in isolation from the presence of its Creator. In the beginning, when God gave life to Adam and Eve, he allowed them to bathe in the light of his presence in paradise. They walked with him and spoke with him. He guided and blessed them in their every action. Alas, soon came the unnatural catastrophe of original sin which shattered the harmony that man enjoyed with his God. It is not that God changed; he remained the same tender Father he had always been, but from that moment on we began to erect walls between ourselves and God. Having lost our knowledge of his goodness, we lost our trust in his love for us.

Ashamed of his sinful condition, man became afraid to try to return to intimacy with his loving Creator, choosing rather to run from his presence: "I heard the sound of you in the garden, and I was afraid, because I was naked; and I hid myself." (Genesis 3:10) This attitude of fear and evasion which we see in the garden also reveals something of how man relates to his own conscience which is the inner ambassador for God. In the moment of the Fall, we became spiritually blind. The absolute knowledge of good and evil which we were seduced into desiring turned out to be a state of intellectual confusion. We lost our knowledge of God, as well as the constant awareness of his omnipresence. The radical folly of denying his existence even became possible for us. In questions of moral and spiritual truth we began to think erroneously, and even became capable of choosing despicable acts of irrational vice. The senses began to dominate, and the marvellous spiritual faculties which make us like God were sunk in the mud of concupiscence.

God did not abandon humanity to its own freely-chosen perversion but continued to reach out to the world at every moment of history. When the divinely appointed moment arrived, the Lord called to himself a chosen people through which he would prepare the world for the coming of Emmanuel, God-with-us. The intimate presence we had enjoyed with God in paradise slowly began to be restored. First, the Lord drew near to Abraham and the patriarchs, speaking directly to them and making promises of joy to come. Then, when the chosen people were exiled in Egypt, God called Moses to lead them out of the land of slavery to a land where they could be free. As they journeyed from one land to the other, they passed through the wilderness, where, upon a mountaintop, God spoke to Moses as one speaks to a friend.

The Return to Intimacy with God

The Lord communicated with Moses through a mysterious thick cloud, which itself marked the place of God's dwelling on earth. (Exodus 24:18) Not that God's presence was confined to any one place but rather that he might begin to prepare the world for a new mode of his presence, what would one day come to be called the Real Presence. The return of Eden's intimacy was fast approaching, but needed preparation. The obstacle to intimacy with God, namely our sinful way of thinking and acting, would have to gradually be removed. Re-education in those commandments of love for God and neighbour which should have always been clearly written in our hearts would now be an essential part of the preparatory covenant. In the restoration of grace to the world, it became God's custom to first send shadows which would act as prefigurations of the realities which he had already pre-determined to send in the fullness of time.

Upon the mountaintop where the commandments were given, the Lord also commanded Moses to construct a tabernacle. In mystical visions, the exact dimensions of this inspired construction were revealed. Moses was told to explain to the people the *raison d'être* of the tabernacle which they were called to help him build: "And let them make me a sanctuary, *that I may dwell in their midst.* According to all that I show you concerning the pattern of the tabernacle, and of all its furniture, so you shall make it." (Exodus 25:8-9) Within the tabernacle there was to be a golden table, about which God said: "And you shall set the bread of the Presence on the table before me always." (Exodus 25:30) To this he added an altar of incense, and an altar of burnt offering, as well as a lamp-stand. Behind the veil, in the holiest part of the sanctuary, Moses installed the Ark of the Covenant within which he placed a jar of the bread from heaven which had fallen from the sky as a sign of God's unfailing providential care. Alongside the manna, he also put the two tables of the law and the rod of Aaron the priest.

The erection of the tabernacle was so important for the chosen people that the Scriptures devote multiple chapters to explaining it all in great detail. Once the tabernacle had been carefully constructed according to the designs which were mystically communicated to Moses, it became the central place of Israel's worship, through which God dwelled among his people. The book of Exodus concludes with the magnificent sight of the carefully constructed tabernacle being filled with the thick cloud, by means of which God approved the work of his people and marked the place of his presence on earth. (Exodus 40:34) The entire exodus had been oriented towards the tabernacle. The contents of the tabernacle would go on to become the Holy of Holies of the Jerusalem Temple. Once that great edifice had been constructed, God also confirmed his presence in the sanctuary by the return of the cloud. (2 Chronicles 5:15)

Interestingly, in the Greek text the verb that describes how the cloud of God's presence overshadowed (*episkiazo*) the tabernacle is the same one that is used to describe how the Holy Spirit overshadowed Mary when the Word became flesh within her womb. (Exodus 40:35, Luke 1:35) This subtle link reveals a profound mystical connection between the old Holy of Holies and the sacred body which Jesus took from Mary. When Saint John tells us that the Word became flesh and dwelt amount us, he literally says that he "tabernacled" among us. (John 1:14) Wherever the body of Christ is present, there is the true tabernacle, the true Temple of God on earth. In order to confirm this to the world, the Father sent his mysterious cloud to overshadow that body once more on the mountain of Transfiguration. (Luke 9:34) The verb used to describe the overshadowing of the cloud is the same as the one mentioned above (*episkiazo*). Just as there was an initial overshadowing of the tabernacle and a subsequent one when it had reached its goal in the Jerusalem Temple of worship, so too, Scripture speaks of an initial overshadowing of the embryonic Christ in Mary's womb, and a subsequent one when his body had come to full maturity and readiness for the Paschal Mystery.

The Gospel of John tells us that Jesus himself spoke of his body as the Temple which would be destroyed and raised again within three days. (John 2:21) Through the tabernacle and the ancient Temple of Jerusalem, God had been slowly helping man to become accustomed to the idea of drawing near to his presence once again. The interior decoration of the Temple contained several garden-like images, showing that the sacred space entrusted to Israel was the beginning of the return to the garden of paradise (1 Kings 6:18-35). There is also a semantic connection between the description of how God once walked with Adam in the garden of Eden and the way in which he was present in the Holy of Holies.[1] In the Incarnation, a whole new level of intimacy with God became possible. God became man so that man might stop running away from him in selfish fear, and come to know his tender kindness once again. With the obstacle of our sins washed away by the blood of the Lamb and our erroneous idea of God transformed by encountering the Person and teaching of Christ, intimacy with the Lord became a reality once again.

It was not only in the Incarnation but above all through the Paschal Mystery that all of this was worked out for us. It is not in his mortal flesh that the Lord chose to remain among us forever, allowing people of all historical epochs to dwell in intimacy with God once again. The joy of his visible bodily presence was granted only to Mary and those who knew him two thousand years ago. In his mortal body he would pass through the agony of death for our salvation and rise anew in a spiritualised body. (Still the body taken from Mary, but now glorious and immortal.) When he spoke of his body as the new Temple, he clearly made a reference to this risen immortal body. (John 2: 19) It is his body in its risen state that is the Holy of Holies on earth where man returns to intimacy with the Godhead. Yet it is not his risen body in its visible condition, but rather in a whole new mode of appearance.

1   Gregory K. Beale, *The Temple and the Church's Mission*, (Leicester: Apollos Publishing, 2004) p.74.

On the night before he died, he held in his sacred hands what looked like bread but what was no longer bread, for Truth himself had just said of it: "This is my body... do this in remembrance of me." He thereby empowered his friends to be able to make his body present in the world after once his Paschal Mystery had been accomplished. As he appeared to St. Mary Magdalene on Easter Sunday, she mistook him for the gardener, thus reminding us of the return of those intimate days when God himself once walked with us in the Garden of Eden. However, he also commanded his witness to the Resurrection not to cling to his body just yet (John 20:17). His risen body is indeed designed to be our contact with paradise while still on earth, but not in its visible form. We must still journey by the darkness of faith, and we must still be free to turn away from that faith. Without freedom there is no merit and no reward. For us the experience of paradise on earth is no longer material but mystical. He would make his body present to us in a Eucharistic mode of appearance which we must gaze upon with the eyes of faith; and once we recognise him there, he no longer says: "Do not cling to me." Through the Eucharistic mystery he invites us to lovingly cling to his sacred body with all of the strength of our soul.

For non-Catholic Christians it must be difficult to understand how Christ's body is the fulfilment of the tabernacle and the Temple. These were liturgical realities, containing mysterious signs like the bread of the presence and the manna from heaven. Only in light of the Eucharistic body of Christ in our tabernacles do we arrive at a true appreciation of how the Old Testament types were destined to be fulfilled. By means of Christ's presence in the Host we are able to live in constant daily communion with him, just as Mary and Joseph did in Nazareth. Saint Joseph was the first person to ever experience the joy of approaching the first "tabernacle" which contained the Real Presence of Christ, and of adoring him when that tabernacle became a monstrance in Bethlehem. She who was both the first tabernacle and the first monstrance would then become Joseph's companion in adoration for all the beautiful years of the hidden life. For them it was the fragility of a poor child's frame which made them shed tears of contemplative amazement; for us it is the frail outward appearance of the species of bread.

Just as the old tabernacle contained a "mercy seat" (Exodus 25:17), so now the new tabernacle is the true throne from which the fountain of mercy flows into the world. Jesus once said as much to Saint Faustina:

"My child, do you fear the God of mercy? My holiness does not prevent Me from being merciful. Behold, for you I have established a throne of mercy on earth —the tabernacle —and from this throne I desire to enter into your heart. I am not surrounded by a retinue or guards. You can come to me at any moment, at any time; I want to speak to you and desire to grant you grace."[1] Purely because of his infinite love for souls, Jesus remains always available in the Blessed Sacrament. If we have a perpetual adoration chapel nearby we can go and look upon him day or night. The consolation of God's perpetually accessible presence which was once the light and joy of paradise is our light and joy once again. As we study the reverent awe with which the people of Israel once approached the Holy of Holies, we learn something of how we should approach the reality in our tabernacles which it foretold.

Original Sin Avenged

The Eucharist is God's radical response to original sin. When J.R.R. Tolkien, a daily adorer of the Blessed Sacrament, wrote his fictional work, entitled *The Silmarillion*, he began it by showing the fall of Melkor. This book was written in order to show the origins or "genesis" of the place called "Middle Earth" which we see at a later stage of its history in the book entitled *The Lord of the*

1   Saint Faustina, *The Diary,* § 1485.

Rings. The fall of Melkor makes us think of the fall of Lucifer, the light-bearer, who became Satan, the accuser. Tolkien conceives creation as a kind of symphony into which Melkor introduces disharmony through his rebellion. Tolkien puts onto the lips of the Creator the following magnificent words about those who would dare to try and bring evil into creation: "For he that attempteth this shall prove but mine instrument in the devising of things more wonderful, which he himself hath not imagined."[1] There is no evil note played into human history which God will not somehow be able to integrate into his great harmonious plan for the salvation of the world. Even the tragedy which was the life of Judas was used by God to bring about the salvation of the whole world. Even the original sin itself has become a *felix culpa,* a happy fault, obtaining for us the joy of Christ's saving presence in the world.

There may be discord for a moment but in the end we will always see what great wonders God devises to overcome it and weave it back into his symphony. Who would ever have imagined that the marvel of the Eucharist would be given to us to put right the separation from God and the division caused by the ancient Fall? Who would ever have imagined that God would become flesh and then go so far as to dwell among us forever in the Blessed Sacrament? As intimately as God dwelled with our first parents in the garden of paradise, he now dwells with us in the garden of the Church. The Eucharist is God's response to the devil's ancient invasion of paradise. For he who dared to bring disharmony into the great symphony of creation has proven to be but God's "instrument in the devising of things more wonderful, which he himself had never imagined..."

The Real Presence of Christ in the Blessed Sacrament is the true wonder of the world, the joy of creation, the high note of the great symphony of all existence! It brings the garden of para-

---

1   J.R.R. Tolkien, *The Silmarillion* (New York: Houghton Mifflin Company, 2004) p. 5

dise back into this valley of tears. Saint Peter Damian was fond of praising Our Lady for giving us the flesh that through the Eucharist has become our glimpse of paradise: "Because of a food we were expelled from paradise, and in virtue of a different food we have been restored to paradise. The food eaten by Eve condemned us to the hunger of an eternal fast; the food given us by Mary has opened the door to the eternal banquet."[2] Our daily lives are far from paradisiacal but thanks to Christ's Real Presence in our midst, we can always retain that inner peace and joy which prefigure those of heaven.

What Christ did for the entire world in his Paschal mystery he does for the individual soul through the Eucharistic mystery. He applies the universal graces of redemption to us in a unique and particular way. In other words, he slowly but surely reverses the consequences of sin and puts the soul back in touch with paradise. The sacrifice of the Mass constantly removes the obstacle to intimacy with God which is caused by our sins. Holy Communion puts us back into union with God and each other, while also repairing the damage caused by sin within our own being. Communion is also the consummation of what should have happened in paradise, in that we now partake freely from the Tree of Life. We took and ate in disobedience in the beginning and this brought eternal death, but now we take and eat in obedience and this brings eternal life. The sword of justice which blocked the way to the fruit of eternal life has been removed by the blood of Jesus and we can now freely consume his risen body which is still the blessed Fruit of Mary's womb. She has become for us the new Tree of Life. Finally, the dimension of Eucharistic presence now allows us to live in a habitual state of intimacy with the Lord once again. Just as he walked in the garden of

---

2   Mother Maria Francesco Perillo, "Mary Coredemptrix and the Eucharist", *Mary at the Foot of the Cross VI*, (New Bedford: Academy of the Immaculate, 2007) p. 233.

Eden with our first parents, so now, he dwells in our midst in the silence of the Blessed Sacrament. As we gaze into the monstrance surrounded by candles upon the altar, we behold the restoration of what was lost in the first book of Scripture and slowly restored throughout the rest of the Bible.

There is one further element of the tragedy of original sin which is also gradually repaired by the power of the Blessed Sacrament. The book of Genesis describes what happened just after Adam and Eve were spiritually poisoned by the forbidden fruit: "*Then the eyes of both were opened, and they knew* that they were naked; and they sewed fig leaves together and made themselves aprons." (Genesis 3:7) In the moment of the first loss of innocence in human history, Scripture tells us that their eyes were opened and that they received a new form of knowledge, but one which leads to death and not to life. Their eyes were opened to sinful realities and closed to divine realities. A disordered curiosity to know and experience what is evil began to infect the human mind, while intellectual clarity on moral and spiritual matters was ruined. The capacity to look upon other human beings as objects to be coveted and used became a real temptation for us.

In the Greek translation of the Bible the words which describe an opening of the eyes and the arrival of a new knowledge appear once again but in an entirely different context. There is perhaps a correlation and a lesson hidden deep within this coincidence of words. On the afternoon of the first Easter Sunday, two men encountered a pilgrim on his way out of the city of Jerusalem. He struck up a conversation with them and journeyed in their company until they arrived in a village called Emmaus. (Luke 24:15) There they invited him to come and eat with them. Although not in his own house, he suddenly became the host! During the course of their meal, this anonymous pilgrim took some bread in his hands and repeated the gestures of the Last Supper with it. As soon as he had handed this bread, which was no longer mere bread, to his hungry fellow pilgrims, he vanished from their eyes, but not before they had the sudden realisation that the pilgrim was in fact the Last Supper host returned from the dead. (We notice that already in the apparitions which take place just after the Resurrection, the substance of Christ's Person is the same, but his outward appearances disguise him.) The Gospel text says that as they took the "bread", their eyes were opened and they recognised him. The "eye-opening" resembles what happened in the Garden of Eden, and the word "recognise" comes from the same root verb for "know" (*ginosko*) which was used in the Genesis text to describe the knowledge resulting from the Fall. (Genesis 3:7) In the Eucharistic encounter with the Risen Lord there is a kind of reversal of what took place in the original sin.

In the moment that our eyes are opened and we first come to recognise the face of Jesus, that is, to truly know that he is present in the Host, the damage done to the mind and heart in the Fall begins to be turned around. Holy desires return to the soul, and the mind begins to penetrate into divine mysteries once again. The conscience begins to regret its covetousness and to seek a holy purity of heart. Moral and spiritual clarity begin to return to the soul through its first vision of Christ's Eucharistic face. For those who doubt that this is true, a simple experiment can be carried out. In any given parish we can ask all those souls who truly believe in and spend time with Jesus is in the Eucharist whether or not they are in agreement with the rest of the Church's teaching on faith and morality. In at least nine out of ten cases, those who "see" Jesus in the Eucharist with the eyes of faith also believe in the other tenets of the Church's faith, and see more clearly what is sinful and what is not. When we meet true adorers, we can be sure that we will not have to argue with them in order to convince them of the evils of abortion, cohabitation, and same-sex marriage, for example. The Eucharistic Lord himself puts this conviction into their hearts when they come to him in faith and adoration. We can also ask them whether or not they personally go to Confession regularly and be quite certain of the response.

The mind and conscience are illuminated by the Eucharistic encounter. If we want to help young people to have the capacity to discern right from wrong, we should bring them to encounter the Lord in the Blessed Sacrament. Once the eyes are opened to see his Eucharistic face by faith and receive him with love, both spiritual and moral insight are also strengthened. The more deeply and more frequently a person gazes into the Blessed Sacrament, the more profound his discernment and moral judgment gradually become. To the one who has perceived Christ's Real Presence in the Host, and who has thus begun to see all of reality in a more truthful manner, the following words could be addressed: "Blessed are the eyes which see what you see! For I tell you that many prophets and kings desired to see what you see, and did not see it, and to hear what you hear, and did not hear it." (Luke 10:23-24)

The Real Presence of Christ Outside the Mass

The most extraordinary Eucharistic prefiguration in the Old Testament, namely, the manna from heaven which we meditated upon in a previous chapter also teaches us something of great importance in relation to the Eucharist as a Presence-Sacrament. The manna would only survive for a day and would then become inedible. If somebody tried to keep extra for the next day, they would find that it had become rotten overnight. (Exodus 16:21) Thus the Israelites learned to trust in God's presence and activity day by day. Through the manna, they learned self-abandonment to divine providence. This is an important lesson for us all.

However, there were two exceptions to this rule, both of which teach us something about the true Eucharistic Manna. First, the manna accommodated itself to the law of the sabbath! As the sabbath day arrived, the manna would survive the night and still be perfectly edible the next day. The sabbath is a foretaste of the rest of the promised land. The Eucharist is a foretaste of heavenly rest and is designed to put us in contact with it already. Our weary hearts find rest in the Sacred Heart. The second exception to the disintegration of the manna was when it was placed in the Ark of the Covenant in the tabernacle.[1] Only in that sacred space could it be preserved long-term (Exodus 16:33). Thus, we see that one of the primary purposes of the manna was to remain present with the people as a perpetual reminder of God's love. The lesson for us is clear: one of the primary ends of the Eucharist is that it be placed in the tabernacle and so become God's Real Presence in our midst. After the Second Vatican Council, some theologians tried to undermine the spiritual instinct of the bride of Christ, by telling her that the Eucharist was designed only to be eaten but not adored. The Church was quick to proclaim the falsehood of this thesis, and the Scripture itself shows us that the manna was made for the tabernacle!

Down through the centuries the Church has penetrated ever more deeply into the three different dimensions of the Eucharist, and none more so than the dimension of presence. Speaking of the intercession which takes place just after the moment of the consecration, when the Lord is present on the altar, Saint Cyril of Jerusalem was already able to say in the fourth century: "We believe that a very great help is granted to the souls for whom we make this prayer, in the very presence of the holy and redoubtable Victim."[2] The Church was obviously already aware that the most privileged place of intercession was in the Real Presence of the Lord. Saint Jean-Marie Vianney repeated a similar truth many

---

1   Brant Pitre, *Jesus and the Last Supper* (Grand Rapids, Eerdmans, 2015) p.154.

2   Charles Journet, *The Mass, the Presence of the Sacrifice of the Cross*. Translated by Victor Szczurek, (South Bend Indiana: St. Augustine's Press, 2008) p. 44

centuries later; it was the fruit of his own experience after having obtained the conversion of countless sinners: "When our Lord is on the altar during Mass, as soon as we pray to Him for sinners, He hurls down towards them rays of light in order to reveal their miseries and convert them."[1] In the Gospels, certain miracles only take place because people have taken the time and effort to come into Christ's living presence. Sometimes these miracles are granted to people who are physically distant from Christ but only because somebody has come into his Real Presence on their behalf (Matthew 15:28). The same power still comes forth from his body in the Blessed Sacrament. Gradually this awareness increased in the Church and the tabernacle became the centre and heartbeat of her life of prayer. The Church was coming to understand what Saint Peter-Julian Eymard would later articulate: "Eucharistic prayer has an additional merit: it goes straight to the Heart of God like a flaming dart; it makes Jesus work, act, and relive in His Sacrament; it releases His power."[2]

The Catechism of the Catholic Church speaks of this development in understanding: "As faith in the Real Presence of Christ in his Eucharist deepened, the Church became conscious of the meaning of silent adoration of the Lord present under the Eucharistic species. It is for this reason that the tabernacle should be located in an especially worthy place in the church and should be constructed in such a way that it emphasises and manifests the truth of the Real Presence of Christ in the Blessed Sacrament."[3] Even more than being the supreme arena for intercession, the Church also began to understand more fully that since Christ is alive in the Host, then Eucharistic Adoration is the place where a reciprocal dialogue of love takes place. Saint Augus-

---

1   *Ibid.* p. 126
2   Saint Peter-Julian Eymard, *The Real Presence* (Cleveland: Emmanuel Publishing, 1938) p. 14.
3   Catechism of the Catholic Church, § 1379.

tine had already said that it was a sin not to adore the Blessed Sacrament before receiving it during Mass, but the Church was slowly becoming aware that adoration of the Eucharist should also take place outside of the Mass.[4] Adoration prolongs and intensifies the grace of the Mass.[5] The same fountain of grace which flows from the altar when Christ is really present upon it at Mass continues to flow day and night when he is reserved in the tabernacle. The Lord began to draw thirsty souls to come and drink deeply from the river of divine love which pours out unceasingly from his Sacred Eucharistic Heart.

Especially through the mystical insights of the saints, the Church grew in her awareness that Christ longs for our love and our presence from his Eucharistic dwelling-place. In the second millennium this awareness was brought to its crescendo. Saint Gertrude and Saint Margaret-Mary Alacoque were instrumental in this development of ecclesial understanding. Saint Francis and Saint Clare had also played their role. Saint Juliana of Mont Cornillon made known Christ's plea for his Real Presence to be appreciated and elevated in the life of the Church. Thus, the feast of Corpus Christi was introduced. Saint Peter-Julian Eymard, the Apostle of the Eucharist, developed an entire spirituality based upon how one should relate to Christ as a real and living Person in the Host. Even in his own devout days of nineteenth century Catholicism, he lamented that there were still too many souls who would treat Jesus in the Blessed Sacrament like a statue. A statue is a wonderful aid to prayer and devotion. Whatever honour we pay to a statue, we somehow pay to the person in heaven whom it represents. But in the Blessed Sacrament the Person in heaven is actually present on earth. We must thus relate to him in his Eucharistic state in the same way that we would have related to him in Galilee two thousand years ago.

4   Saint Augustine, *Enarrationes in Psalmos,* 98:9.
5   Pope Benedict XVI, Angelus, 6th of October 2007.

Saint Teresa of Avila would teach her sisters about the joy she experienced from living with the Eucharistic Lord. Here she speaks of herself in the third person: "The Lord had given this person such a lively faith that, when she heard people say they wished they had lived when Christ walked on this earth, she would smile to herself, for she knew that we have Him as truly with us in the Most Holy Sacrament as people had Him then, and wonder what more they could possibly want."[1] Although Eucharistic Adoration may appear like inactivity, really it is a place of profound and powerful activity. The body of Christ is not a corpse! The Lord in the Blessed Sacrament is alive and active, acting upon us and upon others because of our prayers. Saint Faustina, writing in the twentieth century helped the Church to understand this truth more fully: "When I steeped myself in prayer, I was transported in spirit to the chapel, where I saw the Lord Jesus, exposed in the monstrance. In place of the monstrance, I saw the glorious face of the Lord, and He said to me, What you see in reality, these souls see through faith. Oh, how pleasing to Me is their great faith! You see, although there appears to be no trace of life in Me, *in reality it is present in its fullness in each and every Host.* But for Me to be able to act upon a soul, the soul must have faith. O how pleasing to Me is living faith!"[2]

The Nature of Christ's Presence in the Blessed Sacrament

Nobody did as much to contribute to the flowering of Eucharistic Adoration as the great Saint Thomas Aquinas in the thirteenth century. By means of his intellectual insights into the Eucharistic Mystery, combined with his own personal piety, his influence helped to consolidate the Christian instinct to spend

1 Saint Teresa of Avila, *The Way of Perfection*, § 34.
2 Saint Faustina, *The Diary*. § 1420.

time in adoration of the Blessed Sacrament. Jesus himself is said to have confirmed to the Angelic Doctor that he had indeed understood the Eucharistic mystery as deeply as anybody can while still on earth. At the end of his life, as the Sacred Host was raised before his weary eyes one last time, the saint spoke aloud to the Eucharistic Lord, confessing that for love of him he had studied, kept watch, and toiled. He then left all judgment and correction of his work to the holy Roman Catholic Church.[3] His humble understanding of the role of a theologian in the service of the Church is as much to be commended as his tender love for the living presence of Christ in the Eucharist.

With the aid of Saint Thomas Aquinas we will be able to make some helpful observations about the nature of the Eucharistic presence of the Lord in the tabernacle. The confusion about the nature of Christ's Real Presence which spread throughout the Church in the second half of the twentieth century caused many of the faithful to lose their faith in the Blessed Sacrament. Some may have retained a certain kind of belief in the sacrality of the consecrated species, but this impoverished form of faith is a far cry from what the Church actually believes. Tabernacles were abandoned everywhere and the reception of Communion became woefully irreverent in many places. Thanks largely to the words and example of recent popes the crisis of faith began to be healed to a certain degree and many were led back to the true and orthodox Catholic faith. The reverence of some parish liturgies has not yet caught up with the restored faith of many Catholics, but, little by little, respect is returning. The damage that had been done by erroneous theological ideas could never be completely repaired in an instant, but every day there are souls who discover anew the full stunning truth of the nature of Christ's Eucharistic presence.

3   Charles Journet, *The Mass, the Presence of the Sacrifice of the Cross.* Translated by Victor Szczurek, (South Bend Indiana: St. Augustine's Press, 2008) p. 6.

If poor theology can do so much damage in the Church, then good theology can help to repair it. A brief synopsis of the theological position of Saint Thomas Aquinas on the Eucharist is the perfect remedy to the evils of the past few decades. Saint Thomas was asked to clarify the theological explanation of the Eucharist while he was teaching at the University of Paris. He did so with fear and trembling, terrified that he might weaken the faith of others if he failed to explain the mystery adequately. Once he came to believe that heaven had given its stamp of approval to his thesis while he was at prayer, he went ahead and made it known to the Church. Saint Thomas made use of a term that had already been coined, but which had not yet been fully developed, namely, the term: transubstantiation. It is a term which implies a "compendium of miracles" which serve to make Jesus present in the Eucharist and prolong that unfathomable presence over time.[1] To put it briefly, this term refers to the change which occurs at the moment of the consecration, and by means of which the substance of bread becomes the living substance of Christ's body, and the substance of wine becomes the living substance of his blood. The reality changes while the accidents or appearances remain the same.[2] By using the philosophical

---

1   The term "compendium of miracles" is taken from: Faber, Frederick, *The Blessed Sacrament*, Tan Books, (Rockford, Illinois, 1978) p.57. Although the Eucharist is not like the other visibly verifiable miraculous signs which Christ worked during his life, it nonetheless transcends the ordinary laws of nature. The Real Presence of Christ is wholly supernatural.

2   The Church normally uses the word species to describe the appearances of the Eucharist. The word species is not used in the way it is normally used in the English language, but is taken from the Latin language and simply means outward appearances. Saint Thomas often speaks of accidents rather than species. Accidents are the properties or attributes of a substance. For example, when we say, "John is thin and has black hair", John is the substance, while his weight and hair colour would be accidents. These accidents may undergo change over time, but the substance of John remains the same.

concepts of substance and accidents, Saint Thomas found a way of drawing the human mind as close as it can possibly be drawn to an understanding of the way in which Jesus is really present in the Eucharist.

Since Christ's body is made truly present in the Host, then his blood, his soul, and his divinity must also be present, because these properties of his Person are inseparable from each other. After the consecration, the substance of bread no longer exists, having being replaced by the substance of Christ, yet it is not the custom of theology to speak of the bread as annihilated, since its ceasing to exist does not end in nothingness, but rather in giving way to the Real Presence of Christ.[3] The fact that the accidents of bread remain, even though Christ is fully present in the Host, is a prolongation of the miraculous, since the substance of bread upon which the accidents once depended is gone. From that point onwards, these accidents will be used as the outward signs which indicate where the Lord is truly present on earth and which in themselves also teach us lessons about the mystery of the Eucharist. The outward sign of bread made from many grains demonstrates the unity brought about by this mysterious food. If the accidents were to be broken down or destroyed, the presence of Christ would vanish.

In approaching the Blessed Sacrament exposed in the monstrance, the human senses can only encounter the accidents of bread. What the touch experiences, the eyes see, and the tongue tastes, give the impression that Jesus is not present, but the theological virtue of faith knows that he is there. Occasionally the Lord gives his friends sensible experiences of his Real Presence, thereby confirming what they see with the eyes of faith, but for the most part, the senses are entirely deceived by the Blessed Sacrament. Sensible consolations are sometimes

3   Frederick Faber, *The Blessed Sacrament*, (Rockford, Illinois, Tan Books, 1978) p.57

given at the beginning of an adorer's spiritual journey, so as to fortify faith and prepare the soul for a life dedicated to the Eucharistic Lord. The present author knows of at least one person with a special Eucharistic vocation, whose mission began with a powerful sensible experience of the Real Presence of Christ in the Blessed Sacrament. During a profound encounter with the Eucharistic Lord, waves of heavenly power and love issued forth from the Host in a tangible way.

The conversion story of the daughter of American revolutionary General Ethan Allen, Frances Margaret Allen, bears witness to the extraordinary Eucharistic experiences that are granted to some souls. Although Ethan Allen himself was an anti-Catholic deist, who died in these dispositions when his daughter was just four years old, she went on in later life to become a most fervent adorer. Sent to a school run by nuns in Montreal, at first the irreligious young woman was bold enough to mock the rites of the Catholic faith while there. Then one day a nun told her to carry some flowers to the altar to prepare it for benediction, and to be sure to adore the Blessed Sacrament before entering the sanctuary. While making her way to the chapel she resolved in her heart not to make any such gesture of adoration which she had been told by her family was a form of idolatry. Upon arrival at the gate of the sanctuary she suddenly found herself frozen to the spot. Three times she tried desperately to move, but in vain. In spite of her efforts, she physically could not draw near to the altar. Overawed by what was happening, a feeling of great reverence seized her heart and she dropped to her knees in adoration before the Eucharistic Lord. She was eventually able to arise and gently place the flowers before the altar. She immediately gave her life to Christ, and much to the chagrin of her family, went on to become a devout religious.[1]

1   Louis de Goesbriand, *Catholic Memoirs of Vermont and New Hampshire*, (Press of R. S. Styles, 1886) p.12-28

Some souls are also given the grace to see Jesus in the Blessed Sacrament by means of some kind of vision or infusion of intellectual light. The author knows of at least two souls who underwent extraordinary experiences of this nature which brought them to conversion. The first was a young man from an extremely troubled background, who was invited on pilgrimage to a Marian sanctuary in Europe. While he was there a total stranger came up to him and asked if he wished to know the quickest way to heaven. The man replied affirmatively and was led to a chapel where the stranger proceeded to kneel down and prostrate his head to the floor before the exposed Host. The young man looked down at the stranger and then back up at the Host and saw Christ truly present there. He struggles to describe how exactly he saw him, but he had no doubt from that day forward as to the reality of the Real Presence. He proceeded to prostrate himself as the stranger had done; and a new life began. His existence would be completely transformed as a result of that grace.

Another young woman who had come from Algeria to live in France, having been raised in an extremely strict Muslim family, also had a powerful mystical experience of the Blessed Sacrament. One morning as the bells of the local Church were ringing, she felt an irresistible interior desire to go to the place from which this sound was coming. As she walked into the Church, she saw a group of people on their knees before what looked just like a "golden object" on the altar. In an instant, she received an infusion of grace and saw with the eye of her mind that upon that altar was present the Lord of the world. What she thought was an object was in fact a divine Person. All she could do was fall to her knees and adore. Soon she was giving her testimony before hundreds of young people, trying to make them understand the extraordinary privilege it is to be Catholic and to know the living presence of Jesus Christ in the Eucharist. She can never return to her country as long as she lives, and she has decided to change her name, but she has found the One before whose presence we can say: "One day within your courts is better than a thousand elsewhere" (Psalms 84:10). Her willingness to sacrifice everything for the Blessed Sacrament can only make lukewarm Catholics who downplay Christ's Real Presence blush for shame.

While these graces of sensible experiences, imaginative visions, or even extraordinary external apparitions of the Eucharistic Lord, are certainly possible, and have often been granted to some of the saints at different moments of their lives, they are not the ordinary way in which a human being relates to the Eucharist. Since it is a substantial presence of Christ, which is veiled under visible accidents which do not properly belong to his substance, the presence is only accessible to the eye of the mind; because it alone is the faculty that discerns the substance of things. In general, the intellect takes in information through the senses, processes it with the help of the imagination, and then determines the substance with which it is in contact. The intellect forms categories of substances within itself, by means of which it builds up its ideas and concepts. Normally, when the eye sees an ordinary piece of bread, its accidents of colour and shape are quickly filtered through the senses and the imagination, before the intellect recognises it as the substance of bread. But in adoration, the senses and the imagination are deceived, and they present to the intellect what looks like ordinary bread. However, the faith-filled soul knows better; and this is the reason why the intellect alone can discern the Real Presence of Christ in the Host. The person of faith can certainly make use of the imagination to try and picture the Person of Christ hidden behind the Eucharistic veil, but it is only the spiritual faculties of the intellect and the will that can reach out and perceive his sacred presence.

Saint Thomas Aquinas has an enlightening passage on this subject, in which he explains that the Real Presence of Christ is both *substantial* and *supernatural*. Since it is substantial, it is not accessible to the senses or the imagination which can only perceive accidents. Since it is supernatural, it is not accessible to an intellect which does not have supernatural enlightenment. To the mind of God, the presence of Christ in the Host is as plain as day. To the supernaturally enlightened mind of an angel or one of the blessed in heaven, the Real Presence of Christ is also evident. To the mind of a devout soul on earth, the presence of Christ is known by means of the supernatural virtue of faith. But to an intellect which only has its natural capacities, and no supernatural enlightening by grace, the presence of Christ is not accessible. To the mind of an atheist, there is no access to the Real Presence of Christ. Saint Thomas elaborates: "But it can be seen by a wayfarer through faith alone, like other supernatural things. And not even the angelic intellect by its own natural power is capable of beholding it; consequently the devils cannot by their intellect perceive Christ in this sacrament, except through faith, to which they do not pay willing assent; yet they are convinced of it from the evidence of signs."[1] Since the demons have lost all trace of supernatural grace, not even their angelic intellects are able to penetrate behind the veil to perceive the supernatural presence of Christ in the Host. Yet, because of all the displays of power and grace that have come forth from the Blessed Sacrament down through the ages, they cannot but be certain that Jesus is really present there. What can be said of the devils is more than can be said for some poor "Catholics!"

Really Present?

The question is often asked about whether or not Christ is physically present in the Host. Some theologians respond to this question with such a nuanced explanation that people are

---

1   Saint Thomas Aquinas. *Summa Theologica, Tertia Pars,* Q.76, art.7, Main Body.

left more confused by it than enlightened. Other theologians have sadly steered away from the truth entirely, and through errors like "Transignification" or "Transfinalisation" have veered towards a more Protestant idea of Christ's presence in the Eucharist. A statement by Pope John Paul II in *Ecclesia in America* sheds much light on the true nature of Christ's Eucharistic presence. The pope was distinguishing the different ways in which we can encounter the Lord. Jesus is present in his Word, where two or three are gathered in his name, in his ministers, in the poor... but none of these spiritual modes of presence comes close to the way in which he is really present in the Blessed Sacrament. The saintly pontiff explains: "My Predecessor Paul VI deemed it necessary to explain the uniqueness of Christ's Real Presence in the Eucharist, which "is called 'real' not to exclude the idea that the others are 'real' too, but rather to indicate presence par excellence, because it is substantial". Under the species of bread and wine, *"Christ is present, whole and entire in his physical 'reality', corporally present."*[1]

Since the nature of Christ's Real Presence was being explained in an impoverished manner by some theologians, both Popes Paul VI and John Paul II, sought to reinforce its reality with the strongest language possible. Faced with theologians who were seeking to undermine the truth of the Real Presence, (often as a means of facilitating a false form of ecumenism) some of whom were speaking of it as some kind of vague spiritual presence, not only did the pope use the word "corporal" (bodily), but also the word "physical", to describe its reality. The words were used in order to help the simple believer grasp the fact that the God-Man is fully alive and present in the Host. It is not just that the meaning of the Host has changed, thereby giving it a new spiritual reality—as some compromised theologies were falsely asserting—but rather that the very being of the Host has been changed in the most powerful manner imaginable. The force of the pope's words

---

1   Pope John Paul II, *Ecclesia in America*, § 12. Emphasis added.

was intended to put an end to all clever arguments which, while not explicitly denying the truth of the Real Presence, empty it of any real meaning. The mystery of the Eucharist is incomprehensible, but the Church wants the faith of her children to be in no doubt: our best Friend and Saviour is alive and with us, in the flesh, in every single one of our tabernacles.

Although Christ is truly present in a bodily way in the Host, in all of his "physical reality", as the pope put it, he is present in a manner that differs from the way in which bodies are ordinarily physically present in a given place. His physical presence is real, but it defies the ordinary laws of physics. If a physicist were to examine the Host from a purely scientific perspective, his findings would relate to the species alone. (In the case of Eucharistic miracles, the Lord makes an exception.) The Host makes present the sacred humanity of Jesus, which is seated at the right hand of the Father in glory, but it obviously does not make that glorious presence physically visible in all of its dimensions.

Through the Eucharist, the body of Jesus is really present in our space in a physical manner, but it is present by means of its substance and not in the ordinary way that a body is usually present in a place with all of its visible physical accidents. The Host does not have to be six foot tall in order to contain and veil the human frame of Jesus; nor does its weight correspond to that of a human body. "From which it is evident that the dimensions of the bread or wine are not changed into the dimensions of the body of Christ, but substance into substance."[2] Christ's physical being is present miraculously, but personally and entirely, under a mode of presence which makes him still capable of being our mystical nourishment. Saint Thomas Aquinas uses strong language to describe this for us. He is speaking of the fact that the Eucharist is not just some part of the flesh of Christ, but his entire being:

2   Saint Thomas Aquinas, *Summa Theologica, Tertia Pars,* Q.76, art.1, Reply
     to Objection 3.

"By the power of the sacrament there is contained under it, as to the species of the bread, not only the flesh, but the entire body of Christ, that is, the bones, the nerves, and the like."[1]

Sometimes we hear theologians say that Jesus is not locally present in the Host. We must be careful how we understand this. They are not saying that he is not there, for he is as really present in the tabernacle as he is in heaven.[2] What they are saying is that his mode of presence there differs to all other modes of presence in the universe. There is no other example of presence that can serve to illustrate how the Eucharistic presence works. Ordinarily, a particular body is located in one single place and that same body cannot be present in this way in any other place. We can call our loved ones who live on the other side of the world by telephone, but we cannot be physically present with them while remaining at home. Our bodies would have to change location. In the ordinary order of things, a human body can only be located in one place at a time. Even though Jesus also has only one physical risen body which is located naturally in the glory of heaven, he somehow makes it present here sacramentally without leaving heaven. The Eucharist is not a clone of Jesus, a different Jesus to the One in heaven.

In the Blessed Sacrament, the Lord has found a way of making his one body, which is locally present in heaven, become present in multiple places all at once. At the moment of the consecration, he does not leave one location in order to go and locate himself in another. The American theologian Father James O'Connor, provides a succinct clarification of this truth for us: "In fact, normally speaking, local or physical presence of one person to another is a necessary requisite for the establishment and even maintenance of interpersonal presence. Although not locally present in the Eucharist in the sense of being circumscribed by the

---

1   *Ibid.,* Q.76, art.1, Reply to Objection 2.
2   Frederick Faber, *The Blessed Sacrament,* (Rockford, Illinois: Tan Books, 1978) p. 63.

Host or drawn out of heaven, Christ is truly physically present, and it is precisely that physical proximity that establishes and nourishes interpersonal presence."[3] Interpersonal love is satisfied with nothing less than the physical presence of the beloved. A telephone call, a letter, or a photograph on one's desk, are insufficient. We need to draw near to the heart of the one we love, and this is why Jesus makes his real heart of flesh present to us in the Host. Love has demanded that his physical body be present with us in a real, substantial way. "It is in the nature of man and of his love to require, in order to live, the presence of the object of his love. Love wants to see, to hear, to converse, to touch. Nothing can take the place of the beloved, neither memories, nor gifts, nor pictures; there is no life in these things. Our Lord was well aware of it. Nothing could have taken the place of his Person. We must have our Lord himself."[4]

We do not drag Jesus out of heaven at the moment of the consecration in such a way that his body is no longer in heaven but only here with us. The natural bodily presence of Jesus does not have to abandon the courts of heaven in order to take up residence in the tabernacles of earth. Rather, his one natural body remains present in heaven under its own proper visible appearances, while also making itself sacramentally present under the Eucharistic appearances wherever Mass takes place.[5] When theologians say that Jesus is not locally present in the Blessed Sacrament, they want us to understand that the mode of his presence there is unique. If we were to suddenly move the Host from one place to another, the glorious Saviour in heaven would not be suddenly moved off his throne at the right hand of

3   James O'Connor, *The Hidden Manna*. Ignatius Press, (San Francisco, 1988) p. 161.
4   Saint Peter Julian Eymard, *The Real Presence* (Cleveland: Emmanuel Publishing, 1938) p.76
5   Saint Thomas Aquinas, *Summa Theologica, Tertia Pars*, Q.76, art.5, Reply to Objection 1.

the Father.[1] We move the sacramental species which make his glorious body present in that place on earth. Similarly, because of the uniqueness of his bodily presence, we cannot point to one particular part of the Host and identify there a particular part of the body of Jesus. His presence is far more mysterious than that; mysterious, but real, nonetheless.[2] "In the Eucharist, Christ is truly contained, Body (with all the physical dimensions and members proper to his Body), Blood, Soul, and Divinity, the same Body born of Mary, dead on the Cross, raised gloriously from the tomb. It is not a different Body from the one that "sits at the right hand of the Father", nor is it a part of that Body, nor some kind of amorphous extension of that Body."[3]

By means of his omnipotent divine power, the glorified Jesus can be present to each individual soul who comes to him in the Blessed Sacrament, as though that soul were the only one communicating with him. The Council of Trent tried to put the ineffable divine mystery into human words, just before it proclaimed that the denial of Christ's Real Presence is not just heretical, but also satanical:

> In the first place, the holy Synod teaches, and openly and simply professes, that, in the august sacrament of the holy Eucharist, after the consecration of the bread and wine, our Lord Jesus Christ, true God and man, is truly, really, and substantially contained under the species of those sensible things. For neither are these things mutually repugnant, that our Saviour Himself always sitteth at the right hand of the Father in heaven, according to the natural mode of existing,

1   *Ibid.*, Q.76, art.6, Main Body.
2   Charles Journet, *The Mass, the Presence of the Sacrifice of the Cross.* Translated by Victor Szczurek, (South Bend Indiana: St. Augustine's Press, 2008) p. 162.
3   James O'Connor, *The Hidden Manna* (San Francisco: Ignatius Press, 1988) p. 279.

and that, nevertheless, He be, in many other places, sacramentally present to us in his own substance, by a manner of existing, which, though we can scarcely express it in words, yet can we, by the understanding illuminated by faith, conceive, and we ought most firmly to believe, to be possible unto God.[4]

No matter how many Hosts are in a tabernacle, there is only ever the one same body of Christ made present there. If half of the Hosts are consumed, the one body of Christ remains fully present. If one Host alone remains, the same body is just as equally present. Even if only a single fragment remains in the ciborium, the same body of Christ remains fully present. This is why the *priest* must be careful to purify the sacred vessels slowly and carefully. (I emphasise the word *priest* here, because the purification of the vessels belongs to his ministry—or that of a deacon—and cannot ordinarily be done by a member of the faithful.) The Lord himself explained to Saint Catherine of Siena, who lived on nothing but the Eucharist for the last seven years of her life, the unfathomable mystery of how he is present in every single fragment of the Host:

> *I have said to you that this Body is, as it were, a Sun. Wherefore, you cannot receive the Body without the Blood, or the Blood or the Body without the Soul of the Incarnate Word; nor the Soul, nor the Body, without the Divinity of Me, the Eternal God (…) So that you receive the whole Divine Essence in that most Sweet Sacrament concealed under the whiteness of the bread; for as the sun cannot be divided into light, heat, and colour, the whole of God and the whole of man cannot be separated under the white mantle of the host; for even if the host should be divided into a million particles (if it were possible) in each particle should I be present, whole God*

4   Council of Trent, Thirteenth Session, Chapter I.

and whole Man. When you break a mirror the reflection to be seen in it is not broken; similarly, when the host is divided God and man are not divided, but remain in each particle.[1]

So, the simple answer that we should give to faithful souls—who are not seeking to be theologians, but who simply want to know that the Real Presence of Christ's body is indeed something real—when they ask us whether or not the Incarnate God is physically present in the Eucharist, is: "yes".

The Shock of the Real Presence

In order to better grasp this mysterious presence of Christ in our tabernacles and the response of love which it deserves, we should meditate upon it in the light of his incarnate life on earth. In the moment of the Incarnation everything changed in the relationship between humanity and its Lord. Our Lady who was born with the gift of God's mystical presence within her soul was always absorbed in contemplation of the Godhead. In addition to his mystical presence in her soul, the Eternal Word of the Father through whom all things were created was present everywhere, holding all things in being. Yet, at a certain moment, the Eternal Word became one of us. When the Word was made flesh and took up his bodily dwelling-place on earth, Mary's contemplative gaze had a new visible locus upon which to fix itself. Her adoring heart was called to surround the incarnate heart of God with perpetual love. First she adored that Sacred Heart as it began to beat while still hidden in her spotless womb. Then she would gaze upon him as a child, pondering in her maternal heart everything he said and did, as well as all that others said about him (Luke 2:19). Her adoration continued as that human nature he took within her came to the perfection of manhood, and right through its immolation on

1   Saint Catherine of Siena, *Dialogue*, 3:24.

Calvary and its resurrection from the dead. Her heart kept vigil wherever that sacred body was to be found, for she knew that in him "the whole fullness of deity dwells bodily" (Colossians 2:9).

The apostles too, especially Saint John, were taken into this contemplation of the sacred body of Christ, which alone can reveal the mystery of the Godhead to us. They rejoiced in his Real Presence for the three years of his public life and lamented with bitter tears when they were deprived of that living bodily presence of God in the moment of the Passion. They rejoiced again with celestial happiness when they saw that sacred body risen to its glorious state on Easter Sunday. The apparitions of Christ after the Resurrection can help us to understand how we should relate to his Real Presence in the Eucharist. Saint Mary Magdalene's tears of joy as she glimpsed the face of her Saviour in the Garden of the Resurrection give us some idea. The great Eucharistic theologian Cardinal Charles Journet liked to use Christ's apparitions to the apostles after the Resurrection as a means of describing what he called the "shock" of the corporal presence.[2] The apparition in the twenty-first chapter of the Gospel of John provides a helpful example for us to ponder.

The apostles had already seen Jesus, risen from the dead, and knew that he was mysteriously watching over them still. On this particular morning, they were finishing a fruitless night of fishing on Lake Galilee. Out of the half-light of dawn, a mysterious stranger on the shore directs them to a miraculous catch. By means of his contemplative familiarity with the Person of Christ, Saint John is the first to recognise that the stranger is in fact the Risen Lord. "*Dominus est*", "It is the Lord" he cries out in exultation (John 21:7). Saint Peter is so excited to hear this that he jumps into the water and swims all the way to the Real Presence of his King. In this scene, we pass from a spiritual presence of the Risen Lord to a bodily presence, what we call: the Real Presence.

2   Charles Journet, *Le Mystère de l'Eucharistie,* (Paris: Tequi, 1980) p.70.

The apostles were rediscovering the joy that they had more gently discovered three years earlier, and the joy that Mary had discovered thirty-three years earlier. The shock of the apostles and their amazed reaction to Christ's Real Presence is an example for us of how we should feel when we walk past a Church.

If we really understood the nature of the Real Presence of Christ in the Eucharist we would run with as much excitement as Saint Peter to the adoration chapel. Thankfully, there are always some souls in the world who grasp this truth and treat the Eucharistic Lord as he deserves to be treated. They often end up being canonised! Here is how one of them, the Curé of Ars, described what would happen in his heart whenever he saw a Church: "If we love our Lord, we should have that gilded tabernacle, that house of the good God, always before our mind's eye. When we see a spire from the road, that sight ought to make our hearts beat like the heart of a lover at the sight of the roof under which his love dwells. We ought to be unable to take our eyes off it."[1]

Final Thoughts on the Real Presence

Jesus Christ is in the Blessed Sacrament for our good. He is there because we need him and it would be foolish of us to neglect his presence. In the following chapters of this book we will discuss how we can best respond to the gift of love which is Christ's Real Presence in the Eucharist. For now, we will let Pope Benedict give us a hint. These are the words he addressed to seminarians at the Marian Shrine of Altötting in Germany, upon discovering that they had just turned the ancient treasury into a perpetual adoration chapel:

Eucharistic adoration is an essential way of being with

---

1   Abbé, H Convert, *The Curé of Ars and the Holy Eucharist*, (Minnesota: The Neumann Press, 2000) p. 41

the Lord. Thanks to Bishop Schraml, Altötting now has a new "treasury". Where once the treasures of the past were kept, precious historical and religious items, there is now a place for the Church's true treasure: the permanent presence of the Lord in his Sacrament. In one of his parables the Lord speaks of a treasure hidden in the field; whoever finds it sells all he has in order to buy that field, because the hidden treasure is more valuable than anything else. The hidden treasure, the good greater than any other good, is the Kingdom of God—it is Jesus himself, the Kingdom in person. In the sacred Host, he is present, the true treasure, always waiting for us. Only by adoring this presence do we learn how to receive him properly—we learn the reality of communion, we learn the Eucharistic celebration from the inside. Here I would like to quote some fine words of Saint Edith Stein, Co-Patroness of Europe, who wrote in one of her letters: "The Lord is present in the tabernacle in his divinity and his humanity. He is not there for himself, but for us: for it is his joy to be with us. He knows that we, being as we are, need to have him personally near. As a result, anyone with normal thoughts and feelings will naturally be drawn to spend time with him, whenever possible and as much as possible" (Gesammelte Werke VII, 136ff.). Let us love being with the Lord! There we can speak with him about everything. We can offer him our petitions, our concerns, our troubles. Our joys. Our gratitude, our disappointments, our needs and our aspirations. There we can also constantly ask him: "Lord send labourers into your harvest! Help me to be a good worker in your vineyard![2]

Taking his cue from a few simple words of wisdom from a saintly philosopher, the pope boldly pointed out to these future

2   Marian Vespers with the Religious and Seminarians of Bavaria, Altötting, 11th September 2006.

priests that any Catholic who has a "normal" way of thinking and feeling should be drawn to the tabernacle to spend as much time as possible before our most faithful divine friend. Whoever finds a true friend in this world finds a true treasure and what greater friend could we have than Jesus himself (Sirach 6:4). How the indifference of some souls to the awesome gift of Christ's living presence in the Blessed Sacrament must perplex the angels and saints in heaven. Saint Padre Pio was also perplexed by it while still on earth, especially when he heard of this indifference in the hearts of those who are consecrated to the Lord: "Sometimes I ask myself if there could be any souls who do not feel a divine fire burning in their breasts, especially when they stand before him in the Sacrament. This seems impossible to me, particularly if the souls in question are priests or religious."[1]

---

1   Raniero Cantalamessa, *Words of Light: Inspiration from the Letters of Padre Pio.* (Massachusetts: Paraclete Press, 2008) p. 146.

IV

EUCHARISTIC ADORATION

The Activity of Christ in the Blessed Sacrament

Pope Benedict XVI was a soul who greatly appreciated the joy of Christ's Eucharistic presence. He first discovered it as a boy in Bavaria, when the roads would be lined with thousands and thousands of candles and rose-petals, in order to honour the Blessed Sacrament on the feast of Corpus Christi. There was as much excitement on that day as there would have been for the visit of a Head of State. In the last public homily that he would ever give for the feast of Corpus Christi he left us an insight into his own personal devotion to the Eucharist. It is no secret that Pope Benedict had been deeply troubled by the misinterpretations of the Second Vatican Council in many countries throughout the world. Perhaps no country was more sorely afflicted than his own beloved Germany. Largely because of errors taught by prominent theologians, confusion spread throughout the ranks of the clergy and trickled down into liturgical celebrations of the Eucharist, as

103

well as the spiritual lives of the faithful. Preaching on the Real Presence of Christ in the Eucharist began to fade away and consequently tabernacles remained perpetually abandoned all over the world. Benedict had been present for the providential event of the Council and knew very well that this disrespect for the Eucharist was far from the intention of the Council Fathers. If anything, they were hoping for a great renewal of love and devotion towards the mystery of the Eucharist in all of its dimensions. In his homily for Corpus Christi 2012 the pope wanted to correct the error of certain theologians who were opposed to Eucharistic Adoration.

He first highlights the false notion that Vatican II wanted us to focus on the celebration of Mass alone, and no longer on adoration outside of the Mass. To this theological lie the Pope responded from his own knowledge of the truth of what the Second Vatican Council had really hoped to accomplish:

> *This imbalance has also had repercussions on the spiritual life of the faithful. In fact, by concentrating the entire relationship with the Eucharistic Jesus in the sole moment of Holy Mass one risks emptying the rest of existential time and space of his presence. This makes ever less perceptible the meaning of Jesus' constant presence in our midst and with us, a presence that is tangible, close, in our homes, as the "beating Heart" of the city, of the country, and of the area, with its various expressions and activities. The sacrament of Christ's Charity must permeate the whole of daily life. Actually it is wrong to set celebration and adoration against each other, as if they were competing. Exactly the opposite is true: worship of the Blessed Sacrament is, as it were, the spiritual "context" in which the community can celebrate the Eucharist well and in truth. Only if it is preceded, accompanied and followed by this inner attitude of faith and adoration can the liturgical action express its full meaning and value.*[1]

1   Pope Benedict XVI, *Homily for the Solemnity of Corpus Christi*, 7th of

The pope clearly wanted to put an end to the abandonment of tabernacles throughout the world, so that the Eucharist might be recognised as the "beating Heart" of our cities and parishes. Even further, the wise man of God saw clearly now that the attempt to focus only on the Real Presence of Christ during the Mass actually destroyed the very thing it purported to desire. In other words, if people do not adore the Eucharistic Lord outside Mass it is very difficult for them to adore and have a personal encounter with the same Eucharistic Lord during Mass. The Mass moves along quite quickly and if people have not cultivated the grace of recollection and attentiveness to the Real Presence of Christ in silent prayer outside of Mass, it is very difficult for them to suddenly conjure this up during the Mass. The loss of the spirit of Eucharistic Adoration means that very soon Christians lose sight of the fact that the Mass is an act of adoration, the highest act of adoration. If we do not discern the Person of Christ in the Sacred Host in silent loving adoration, we will not be able to discern the presence of the same Person just before we receive Holy Communion. This is why Pope Benedict also asked that children be formed in Eucharistic Adoration before they make their first Holy Communion.[2] If they have been helped to adore the Real Presence of Christ in the Host, then they will approach Communion with at least some sense of awe and wonder. A person who made a good first Holy Communion in childhood will never ordinarily suffer the complete loss of Eucharistic faith. "A child may despise his father and insult his mother, but it is impossible for him not to recognise them. In the same way, a Christian cannot deny that he has communicated; he cannot forget that he was happy at least once."[3]

June 2012.

2   Pope Benedict XVI, *Sacramentum Caritatis*, § 66.

3   Saint Peter Julian Eymard, *The Real Presence* (Cleveland: Emmanuel Publishing, 1938) p. 50.

In the same homily for Corpus Christi, Pope Benedict goes on to respond to the error of those who oppose Eucharistic Adoration, not so much from a theological or magisterial perspective, but rather from his own experience of a life spent in constant communion with the silent God of the Eucharist:

> *The encounter with Jesus in Holy Mass is truly and fully brought about when the community can recognise that in the Sacrament he dwells in his house, waits for us, invites us to his table, then, after the assembly is dismissed, stays with us, with his discreet and silent presence, and accompanies us with his intercession, continuing to gather our spiritual sacrifices and offer them to the Father.*[1]

This last statement is worthy of meditation and resembles a thought that could be found in the spiritual teachings of the greatest of Eucharistic saints. Day and night, Jesus in the Blessed Sacrament is calling us to himself. He is perpetually interceding for us before the Face of God the Father. He is uniting our "spiritual sacrifices" to himself, purifying them and offering them to the Father on our behalf. Rarely has a magisterial statement spoken with such clarity about the living, personal presence and activity of Jesus in the Blessed Sacrament. Only a few months before he devoted the rest of his life to prayer alone, the holy pontiff gave the Church a little glimpse into his own spiritual life, and pointed out to us the path to holiness, the path to heaven. It is the luminous path of deep and constant intimacy with the living Eucharistic Heart of Jesus.

Why expose the Blessed Sacrament?

If Christ is alive and active in the tabernacle then why is exposition necessary? Why do people always long to make the Host

---

1 Pope Benedict XVI, *Homily for the Solemnity of Corpus Christi*, 7th of June 2012.

visible, rather than just adore Jesus in the tabernacle? This question often arises. It usually comes up most frequently in circles of people who are guided more by their head than by their heart. This is not a criticism. Some people are naturally more intellectually absorbed than others, and feel the need to analyse everything. For habitual adorers there is generally no question about it, they long to gaze upon the Lord Jesus in the monstrance and will often travel many miles just to do so. This spiritual instinct cannot be erased from their hearts by clever arguments and they have the intuition that once the Lord is exposed everything changes.

Power seems to go forth from his sacred body more abundantly when he passes from his "hidden life" in the tabernacle to his "public life" in the monstrance! Saint Peter-Julian Eymard spoke to his religious sisters of this sentiment which consumes the heart of those called to a specifically Eucharistic vocation: "You yourselves, if you go on a voyage, do not know how to pray in the churches any more, yet our Lord is present there, but it is not your radiant and glorious Jesus as the Church gives him to you to honour by the solemn cult of exposition. I tell you that when you were created, the Father said to His Son, 'Here is an adorer for you.'"[2]

In order to answer this question about whether or not we should expose the Blessed Sacrament, we could have recourse to theological reasoning, based upon theories like the one which holds that the human soul absorbs information only through the senses, and thus the visibility of the Host enhances the interior experience of adoration. However, instead of turning to theological reasoning, I have thought it best to offer readers a different kind of reasoning, the reasoning of a child. Her name is Nellie Organ, also known as "Little Nellie of Holy God." Although generally considered by the Irish to be a saint, she is not yet beati-

2   Saint Peter Julian-Eymard, *The Eucharist and Christian Perfection II*, (New York: The Sentinel Press, 1948) p.27.

fied; but, then again, such a marvellous little angel scarcely needs beatification. Her pure soul left this world while she was still in her fifth year, already ablaze with love for the Blessed Sacrament.

Born in County Cork and orphaned as a baby, Nellie went to live at an orphanage run by religious sisters. As soon as she could speak, the precocious infant began to demonstrate an unusually clever mind and wit. She would weep bitterly upon hearing about the Crucifixion.[1] Above all, she began to manifest an intense love for the Blessed Sacrament. Her preferred name for Jesus was "Holy God" and she would often ask why Holy God was always in the "lock-up?" This was her sweet perplexity at the fact that the Prisoner of Love was rarely "released" for a day and placed in the monstrance. As time went by the "Little Violet of the Blessed Sacrament", as some have called her, seemed to be having mystical experiences. Her thirst to receive Holy Communion was so intense that she would weep bitter tears during Mass. The religious sisters, feeling that it would be irreligious to ignore the daily pleas for Communion from a suffering child, eventually asked the bishop to come and interview her for himself.

In the meantime, Nellie had become too sick from tuberculosis to go from the orphanage to the chapel on a regular basis. Her only comfort would be that the nanny who cared for her would receive Holy Communion and then come to make her thanksgiving beside Nellie's bed. This would allow the little one to rest on the woman's lap and be as near as possible to Holy God for at least a few minutes. On one occasion, the lady was unable to make it to Mass but was afraid to tell Nellie because this would cause her even more suffering. When she arrived at her bedside, Nellie asked if she had been to Mass. The nanny said that she had, to which Nellie replied: "You did not get Holy God today."[2] We may not be

---

1   The Good Shepherd Sisters, *The Life of Little Nellie of Holy God*, (Charlotte: Tan Books, 2013) p.3.
2   *Ibid.* p.35.

always aware of the fact that we are true tabernacles during those fifteen minutes which follow Mass, but the angels and those with angelic hearts can perceive it. Little Nellie would also reverently touch the lips of others who had just received Holy Communion.

What amazed the sisters and their staff in the orphanage the most was the fact that Nellie would know, without being told and while still in her little bed, when Jesus was exposed in the Blessed Sacrament in the convent chapel. She would awaken with a burst of excitement and exclaim: "Holy God is not in the lock-up today, take me to the chapel!"[3] Her fragile little body would suddenly find a new lease of life and summon the strength necessary to go and gaze upon the living Host in the monstrance. The look on her face in adoration was described as "ecstatic" or "transfigured." For Little Nellie there was obviously a huge difference between keeping Christ hidden in the tabernacle and allowing the Eucharistic Lord to be seen in adoration.

When the bishop finally came to question the four-year-old and saw the intensity of her desire for Holy Communion, as well as her stunning insights into the mysteries of the faith, he made an exception which was very rare in those days and decided to give the child Holy Communion. The priest who was privileged enough to administer the Host to her later testified to the fact that all who were present felt as though light were shining from her countenance, and that she seemed to remain in a silent ecstasy after receiving the Lord.[4] She was bathed in peace for the rest of the day. Shortly after her first Communion her little soul took flight for the courts of heaven. The sinful world could hold this innocent Eucharistic angel no longer. Her life-story was taken by Pope Pius X as one of the signs that the age of first Holy Communion was to be lowered. In order to explain the mystery of her short Eucharistic life, we could paraphrase the

3   *Ibid.* p.36.
4   *Ibid.* p.56.

book of Wisdom: Being perfected in a short time, she fulfilled long years; for her soul was pleasing to the Lord, therefore he took her quickly from the midst of wickedness (Wisdom 4:13-14).

What is Adoration?

The writings and sermons of Pope Benedict XVI contain many beautiful insights about the Eucharist, and there is one which will help us to understand the nature of Eucharistic Adoration before moving on to a study of adoration in the lives of the saints. In order to explain this form of prayer to the young people gathered for World Youth Day in 2005, the Pope analysed the root meaning of the word adoration. In Greek the word for adoration is *proskynesis*, which gives us the idea of submission before the omnipotence of God. We can think of the many instances of adoration in the Old Testament, where God drew his people to an awareness of his divine majesty and they would fall prostrate before him, representing the total submission of their lives to his divine power. The instinct of the ancients to offer sacrifice to God from their first fruits was an expression of adoration. They knew that in justice, we owe God a debt of gratitude, which we express by adoring him.

Ultimately adoration leads us to make of our entire lives a living sacrifice for God, which itself is expressed by seeking to do his will. The proper disposition of a creature is to do the will of its Creator, and in adoration we should expose our souls to the Lord in such a way that we sincerely desire that his will be done. We lay down our lives before him. The Blessed Virgin Mary in the moment of the Annunciation offers us an example of the attitude of the perfect adorer. Christ in his agony in the Garden of Gethsemane, offers us another. "...Not my will, but yours be done" (Luke 22:42). In that same homily, the Pope also looked at the word for adoration in Latin. He said: "the Latin word for adoration is *ad-oratio*—mouth to mouth contact, a kiss, an embrace, and hence, ultimately love. Submission becomes union, because He to whom we submit is Love. In this way submission acquires a meaning, because it does not impose anything on us from the outside, but liberates us deep within."[1]

This second way of understanding adoration by looking at the Latin word for it is very important for those who wish to understand Eucharistic Adoration in particular. Adoration is a reciprocated exchange of love which passes between the soul and the One who is Love. In the Eucharist we truly encounter Jesus Christ, the Eternal Word enfleshed. Our faith tells us that the God of all power and majesty, before whom Moses and the People of Israel trembled in awe, assumed our own human nature and walked the face of the earth. In the Person of Jesus Christ we have come to understand that the Creator God, whose name was too holy to be mentioned for the people of Israel is a God of purest love. The God before whom Moses removed his sandals in fear, would one day take the "form of a slave" and after removing the sandals of his apostles, would humbly wash their feet (Phil 2:7).

It is wonderful to meditate upon the loving abasement of Almighty God in the Person of Jesus Christ. In the Eucharist this Incarnate God is still alive and present in the world; and in the Eucharist the abasement and love of God have been taken to the furthest possible extreme. The God who hides himself behind the poverty of the Eucharistic veil does so in order to prove to us the infinite love of his Sacred Heart. This is why adoration must have these two dimensions of submission and love. There must be a humble laying down of our entire lives before the Eucharistic Lord. We must approach him with the utmost reverence, but we must also approach him with hearts filled with love. Our desire must be to respond to the infinite love of the Heart of Christ, with the gift of our own love. Adoration must ultimately lead to the union of two hearts.

1   Pope Benedict XVI, Homily for World Youth Day 2005.

Perpetual Eucharistic Adoration

We live during a time of extreme spiritual warfare! As the Church Militant continues her pilgrimage through the darkened world, on her way to the luminous homeland of heaven, her path is strewn with the obstacles and snares set by the enemy. Just as the chosen people of Israel were often assailed by enemies from every side, so too the Church is assailed by spiritual enemies. Just as the victory against the Amalekites was obtained first and foremost through intercessory prayer, so too, the Church must obtain the power to conquer her foes through intercession before the Eucharistic Lord (Ex. 17:11). Moses could not interrupt his strenuous act of intercession on the mountaintop until the battle was over, and the Church cannot interrupt her Eucharistic Adoration until history reaches its consummation in the marriage of the Lamb. At every moment, somebody must be interceding before the Lord. Saint Peter-Julian Eymard clearly grasped this truth. He exposed the Blessed Sacrament in the middle of the nineteenth century and desired that it remain exposed until the end of time. In the same century there were also other holy religious who received a similar insight. Towards the turn of the century, Mother Adele Garnier was shown by Jesus himself that he wanted to be adored perpetually on the hill of Montmartre in Paris.

A little-known saintly woman of the Eucharist, Mother St. Joseph, the nineteenth century foundress of the Franciscan Sisters in Drumshanbo, Ireland, received a similar instruction to that given to Mother Adele. She was the privileged recipient of several apparitions, as well as certain ecstatic experiences just after Holy Communion. Jesus told her that he wanted her community to start a perpetual Eucharistic Adoration that would run until the end of time. Her life confirms the fact that perpetual adoration is one of the spiritual weapons given us for the spiritual combat in which we find ourselves. Jesus let her see the extraordinary fruits for the entire world that would eventually come through perpetual intercession before the monstrance. She described to one of her sisters the nature of the communication which she had received from the Lord:

Our Divine Lord wished the Devotion to the Most Blessed Sacrament to be increased over the whole world; that we were to have Perpetual Adoration and Exposition of the Most Blessed Sacrament in our Convent Chapel; that we should be the Adorers to keep watch, hour by hour, day and night, before the Most Holy; that a high Tower should be built, and that the Bell should toll every hour, one, two, three; and that men's hearts should be touched thereby; that ladies would furnish the pecuniary aid necessary for the Perpetual Adoration which implied Exposition. (...) Our Divine Lord also spoke about the Churches of Ireland -- that poverty prevented the Blessed Sacrament being reserved in the Tabernacle [in many cases]; but He wished His priests to be zealous about the adornment of their churches and altars; that his consecrated spouses, also, were to be zealous for the adornment of the Sanctuary, and that they would thus minister to Him personally. No heed should be paid to those who murmured against what they would term 'this waste,' as the Pharisees had murmured that the price of the precious ointment was not given to the poor. (...) Our Divine Lord again made known to our dear Mother St. Joseph that great blessings would descend upon our country through means of Devotion to the Most Blessed Sacrament -- that external demonstrations and the decoration of Churches honoured Him, and that even regal honours should be paid Him as a King upon His Throne in the Sacrament of His Love; that poverty was not the virtue most necessary to preach now, as in the time of Francis; but devotion to the Blessed Sacrament and the Passion, and that whoever honoured these two great mysteries the most would be first in his sight.[1]

The fruits of perpetual intercessory prayer before the Blessed Sacrament have the power to effect epochal changes in the Church and the world. "Prayer joined to sacrifice constitutes the most powerful force in human history."[2] There is no better sacrifice than giving up the pursuit of other things so as to come before the Eucharistic Lord. This is one penance that will change the world. Yet, it does not remain penitential for long, because soon we begin to prefer adoration to any other activity! Pope Saint John Paul II once said that when we engage in Eucharistic Adoration, we are there on behalf of those who are far from God and do not know him.[3] We might say that we are there in the name of the one who is most in need of God's mercy at that particular moment. Since there are souls dying at every moment, it is important that there are other souls before our Lord obtaining the grace of mercy for them. Even a life badly lived can end well, provided that repentance and grace are accepted.

Perpetual Eucharistic Adoration was carried out faithfully by many religious orders throughout the nineteenth and twentieth centuries. Sadly, many of these communities began to lose vocations in the late 1960's and the chain of uninterrupted perpetual Eucharistic intercession began to be broken. Then something wonderful occurred. The lay faithful were called into the battle and parishes began to organise perpetual adoration. This new grace for the Church coincided with the arrival of Saint John Paul the Great in Rome. Laypeople began to take up what was lost

1   Thomas Concannon, *At the Court of the Eucharistic King* (Dublin: Gill and Son Co., 1929) p. 127-129.
2   Pope John Paul II, General Audience, January 12, 1994.
3   Pope John Paul II, Letter To The Bishop Of Liège On The Feast Of Corpus Christi, May 28, 1996.

by the religious. The gates of hell will never prevail! There had been some nocturnal adoration societies in the past, as well as occasions of the forty-hour devotions in parishes, but now a wave of perpetual adoration began to sweep across the whole world. What was revealed to Mother St. Joseph in Drumshanbo now began to be felt as a calling by many parishes. The Church in the United States was at the forefront of this mission to adore the Lord perpetually. After several decades of perpetual adoration, we can be sure that there are now many Eucharistic saints in our midst.

Soon the magisterium of the Church was voicing its appeal to keep the Blessed Sacrament surrounded by faithful and continuous devotion. In addition to the need for intercession, there is also a simple need to respond to the perpetual presence and love of Christ in the Eucharist. He thirsts for our love and he deserves to have his bride forever before his face. The Real Presence of Christ is worthy of the Real Presence of the faithful. Pope John Paul II had already done much for the spread of perpetual Eucharistic love, instituting all-day silent adoration in the major basilicas of Rome, and in the Shrine of the Divine Mercy in Poland. At the Eucharistic Congress in Seville in 1993, he was moved by the perpetual chain of adoration which went on day and night during the days of the congress. In the closing homily he expressed his desire to see that permanent adoration continue and that every single parish would have at least some adoration.[4] Pope John Paul stopped short of officially asking for the establishment of adoration, day and night, in dioceses throughout the Universal Church. Pope Benedict would be more explicit in his requests.

The year 2007 was a time of great grace for those who love the Eucharist. During that year Pope Benedict published his magnificent exhortation on the Eucharist called *Sacramentum Caritatis*. In this document the Pope gave us a beautiful catechesis

4 Pope John-Paul II, Homily for the 45th International Eucharistic Congress, Seville, June 12, 1993.

on the Mass and Eucharistic Adoration, and asked explicitly that chapels of perpetual adoration be established all over the world, especially in densely populated areas.[1] This momentous request from the Vicar of Christ was another clear sign of the remedy that the Holy Spirit is giving us in order to overcome the current crisis in the Church. During the same year, on the feast of the Immaculate Conception, the Congregation for the Clergy wrote to all bishops asking them to establish sanctuaries of perpetual Eucharistic Adoration in every diocese in the world, as well as the dedication of priests to the ministry of promoting adoration. The main goal of this initiative was to bring about the sanctification of the clergy and to obtain new and holy vocations. The Church desired to offer up an unceasing Eucharistic prayer of petition all over the world so as to bring about a renewal of the sacred priesthood.

Perpetual Eucharistic Adoration is not a purely private devotion, but an ecclesial mission. Since the Church has specifically requested this grace, she has officially commissioned her children to carry out the task. It is thus something which belongs to the public life of the Church. When a parish launches perpetual adoration, with the blessing of the local ordinary and the local pastor, the faithful are entrusted with a mandate from the Church. They are no longer there in a simple role of personal devotion, but participating in a chain of intercession which cannot be broken. They are members of a great team, an army of adorers, waging war against the powers of darkness that menace our world. They are there in the name of their own family members, their spiritual family members in the parish, as well as the entire family of humanity. Perpetual Eucharistic Adoration is one of the greatest acts of charity which we can carry out for the world. "Through adoration, the Christian mysteriously contributes to the radical transformation of the world and to the sowing of the

1 Pope Benedict XVI, *Sacramentum Caritatis* §67.

Gospel. Anyone who prays to the Saviour draws the whole world with him and raises it to God. Those who stand before the Lord are therefore fulfilling an eminent service. They are presenting to Christ all those who do not know him or are far from him: they keep watch in his presence on their behalf."[2]

While we give thanks to the Lord for the graces he pours out through perpetual adoration, we must, nonetheless, try to come to Jesus in the Eucharist for pure motives, simply because his presence is worthy of our time. We must never "instrumentalise" the presence of the Lord, only going to him to obtain the things we desire. This is not love. If a person sought to marry a wealthy person simply because he would obtain things from the marriage, we would clearly recognise that this is not true love. Jesus calls us to respond to his love with love, and not to "use" him just for blessings. Yet, because of his generosity, there will always be great benefits and graces which come as a result of the time that we spend in his presence. For Saint Peter-Julian Eymard the establishment of solemn perpetual adoration in a place is the establishment of a new throne from which Christ will direct us to do his will and from which he will take up his reign of love in many souls. "What a sublime mission it is to be the archangels of his Eucharistic royalty, to be sent by him as messengers of his grace, to kindle a new flame, to erect a new throne, to conquer a new kingdom for him!"

---

2   Pope John Paul II, *Letter To The Bishop Of Liège On The Feast Of Corpus Christi*, May 28, 1996, §5.

V

SEVEN SAINTS OF THE BLESSED SACRAMENT

All of the saints are Eucharistic saints, but some more than others are entirely characterised by their attachment to the living presence of Jesus in the Blessed Sacrament. There are so many of them to choose from, but I have selected seven holy men and women who manifest something of the different dimensions of grace available to those who let their lives unfold in the light of the monstrance. Some of them are not yet canonised, but their lives are already considered as examples of holiness to follow. For those of them who are not well-known some short biographical information will be provided.

Saint Jean-Marie Vianney
Apostle of Eucharistic Preaching

"*Il est là!*", "He is there!" This was the famous line that the holy Curé of Ars never ceased to repeat to his parishioners, as he pointed to the tabernacle during his homilies. Often, when he began to speak of the Eucharist he was so moved that he could not finish the sermon.[1] His tears made up for what was left unsaid. Saint Jean-Marie Vianney is the model of parish priests and as such he teaches us that the lives of priests should be entirely centred on the Real Presence of Christ in the tabernacle. Towards the end of his life he hardly ever preached a homily without referring to the hidden presence of Christ in the Eucharist.[2] His method of reading the Gospels consisted of applying what is said there about Jesus to the Blessed Sacrament. What the Lord began to do for the world two thousand years ago, he continues to do for every generation through the Eucharist.

The holy Curé handled the Host and looked upon the tabernacle with such reverent awe that his parishioners were magnetically drawn to Jesus. He did not have to try and coax his parishioners to come to adoration. He looked at the Blessed Sacrament with such love that the people could not but look there in a similar way. Since he himself spent so many hours before the Blessed Sacrament each day, his example soon enkindled such a fire of Eucharistic love in Ars that it still burns to this day. There is now a perpetual adoration chapel in what was once the little orphanage established by Saint Jean-Marie. He used to organised long chains of adoration for those poor little children, especially during times of serious need. Today, the parishioners continue to sustain an uninterrupted chain of adoration on that very spot. This Eucharistic witness of love is the one that holy Mother Church gives to her priests as the one to imitate. A priest's joy is found in nothing worldly but in Christ alone. All priests should share in the wonder that the Curé expressed at being able to hold Jesus in his hands each day: "In times of discouragement, when

---

1   Abbé, H. Convert, *The Curé of Ars and the Holy Eucharist*, (Minnesota: The Neumann Press, 2000) p. 19
2   *Ibid.* p.32

after the Consecration, I hold in my hands the most holy Body of our Lord, seeing myself to be only worthy of hell, I say to myself: Ah, if only I could take him with me! Hell would be sweet near him (…) But then there would not be any more hell: the flames of love would extinguish those of justice." [3] His attitude towards the Eucharist resembles that of Saint Veronica Giuliani who used to be astonished that priests could hold Jesus in their very hands and not lose their minds with the intensity of the love. She would often experience the bliss of heaven as soon as the Host was placed upon her tongue.[4]

However, we must not be under the illusion that all was rosy in the mission of the Curé of Ars to convert his lukewarm parish. In the beginning, the results of his efforts were slow to emerge. The people were hardened and at first indifferent to his holiness and his words. Some were even irreverent while in the Church. While other priests might have yielded to discouragement, Saint Jean-Marie, like a great military general chose to adopt a different strategy. It was then that the holy priest had recourse to the twofold invincible weapon of penance and prolonged prayer. Fasting and vigils became his very way of life. He threw himself at the feet of the Eucharistic Lord and with tears he begged for the conversion of souls. His resolution to stop at nothing to convert his parish was a turning-point for the entire Church in France. The moment is described for us in the beautiful book entitled: *The Curé of Ars and the Holy Eucharist*: "How much the uselessness of his ministry among the population where he was to spend his life must have filled him with sadness! That sorrow, however, never went as far as faint-heartedness. Fully recognising the difficulty of the enterprise, M. Vianney believed

3   *Ibid.* p. 18
4   Mother Maria Francesca, Perillo, "Mary Coredemptrix and the Eucharist", *Mary at the Foot of the Cross VI*, (New Bedford: Academy of the Immaculate, 2007) p. 251.

that he would succeed by his prayers, sighs, and groaning before our Lord. From that time he resolved to consecrate his days and nights to entreating the divine mercy to act itself on the hearts of his parishioners, and he chose the Church for his dwelling. He might be seen prostrate for long hours on the pavement of the choir, utterly motionless. There he recited a great part of his office, without any support whatsoever; his chest, wasted with fasting, heaved with long sighs, and he paused often, and gazed at the tabernacle with eyes wherein such vivid joy was portrayed, that one might have believed that he saw our Lord, and which made his parishioners say: 'Our curé is a Saint.'"[1]

Soon a small trickle of penitents began to flow back to the confessional. Soon the trickle became a stream and before long it was a torrent. Once the momentum had begun, nothing could stop it. His reputation for sanctity was broadcast far and wide. Not only did he obtain from the Eucharistic Heart of Jesus the conversion of his entire parish, but also the conversion of thousands who flocked to him from all over the country and beyond. He had no great skills of eloquence to mesmerise the crowds, no elaborate pastoral strategies to assist him, but won his battle for souls with the ever reliable methods of adoration, penance, and long hours in the confessional.

Any priest who works such wonders for the Lord can expect the attacks from the enemy to come thick and fast. The Curé was no exception. He was constantly beset by the mind-games played by the enemy to frighten or discourage him into putting an end to his warfare. On the morning that he started the Forty Hours Eucharistic devotion in his parish his bed was set on fire.[2] On other occasions his bed would be shaken by the evil spirits who hurled at the saint their cruel insults and threats. They would

---

1   Abbé, H. Convert, *The Curé of Ars and the Holy Eucharist*, (Minnesota: The Neumann Press, 2000) p. 114.
2   Ibid. p. 70

continually try to disturb the very small amount of sleep he had allowed himself, so as to push him to a mental breakdown. His malevolent spiritual persecutors even went so far as to mock him for the fact that his daily diet consisted of nothing but a poor potato: "Vianney, Vianney! potato eater!, you are not dead yet! I shall get you alright!"[3]

The man of God was unmoved by the intimidation, often laughing it off, and with great trust in the help of the Lord and his holy Mother continued the march to conquest undeterred. When the enemy cannot tempt a soul to sin or capitulation, he then goes to work by attacking it through people who have opened the door to his activity by their own sins. Yet, even these attacks are turned to good by the Lord. They serve to deepen and manifest the strength of the virtues contained in a saintly soul. The Church did not canonise Saint Jean-Marie simply because he worked miracles or because he could read souls in the confessional and remind them of certain grave sins they may have left unconfessed. Rather, she canonised him because he was filled with humility and charity. Story after story from his life manifest the depth to which these two virtues had firmly planted themselves in his soul. These virtues enabled him to conquer even the hardest of hearts for Christ. He once wrote to thank a priest for his honesty, after the priest had told him bluntly of his theological ignorance. The same priest, recognising his pride and lack of charity, immediately walked to Ars and fell at his feet in tears.[4] These disarming and irresistible virtues came to him from the Eucharistic Lord. In the long hours he spent before the transfigured body of Christ in the Blessed Sacrament, the Curé was also transfigured by that same light. His luminous witness to the power of Eucharistic

3   George Rutler, *The Curé d'Ars Today*, (San Francisco: Ignatius Press, 1998) p.173.

4   George Rutler, *The Curé d'Ars Today*, (San Francisco: Ignatius Press, 1998) p.184.

Adoration, by means of which he obtained the grace to convert his entire parish, offers all priests the foundation of the pastoral program they should follow.

Saint Peter-Julian Eymard
Apostle of Eucharistic Spirituality

The great Saint Peter-Julian Eymard, known as the Apostle of the Eucharist, was a contemporary and friend of the holy Curé of Ars, who encouraged him to follow the path of his Eucharistic vocation. When struggling with the foundation of the Blessed Sacrament Fathers years later, Saint Peter-Julian went to the parish of Ars to invoke the intercession of his saintly friend. The holy Curé is said to have burst into tears because Father Eymard, who had the privilege of spending his life before the monstrance, was coming to ask him for prayers.[1] At this point Saint Jean-Marie was spending up to fifteen hours a day in the confessional and no longer had the joy of being able to pray as much as he would have liked to. He had become a prisoner of the confessional, condemned by his own reputation for holiness to decades of hard labour. The tears he wept upon hearing of the evil hidden in the hearts of men had become his daily bread. If the Curé could ever have been tempted to envy anybody it would have been Father Eymard. How he longed to live a life similar to his own, a life which is the beginning of heaven on earth, a life of perpetual Eucharistic Adoration. When Saint Eymard saw the tears he had provoked in the poor man of God, he himself began to weep too. After his departure, the holy Curé solemnly declared to a friend: "Father Eymard is a great saint!"[2]

This great Eucharistic saint was drawn to the Blessed Sacrament from his earliest years. While still in his mother's womb, he

---

1   André Guitton, *Peter Julian Eymard, Apostle of the Eucharist* (Montreal: Pauline Publishing, 1992) p. 163.

2   *Ibid.*, p.140.

was already bathing in the light of the monstrance, as his devout mother would be regularly present for Eucharistic Adoration and Benediction. Like a new Saint John the Baptist, he drew near to Jesus while still in the womb, and as soon as he could talk he was already bearing witness to the same Lamb of God. When he was four or five years old he went missing in the little village of La Mure, at the foot of the magnificent Alpine mountain where Our Lady of La Salette would soon appear. After a long search, his sister eventually tracked him down in the parish Church which is still standing to this day. He had climbed up on the high altar and was kneeling with his ear pressed to the door of the tabernacle. When his distraught sister asked him what on earth he had been doing in climbing up there, he replied: "I can listen to Him better from here."[3] On the day of his first Communion, he whispered to Jesus in his heart: "I shall be a priest, I promise you." Even thirty years later he could not recall this event without tears.[4]

The child was destined from all eternity to become the Apostle of Eucharistic Adoration. When he first began his trademark "Eucharistic preaching" in the city of Toulon, he was like an angel of fire, come to earth with a new revelation of the Eucharist for the world. His words flowed like streams of light and fire.[5] He was aware of the need to preach constantly on the truth of the personal presence of Christ in the Eucharist. The need for this new Eucharistic Evangelisation is even more pronounced in our own days, when faith and love have grown cold in so many hearts. "It is no longer a question of defending a truth of the faith, but of defending the King of truth who is under attack everywhere; nor of professing an evangelical virtue, but of serving Our Lord

3   Albert Tesnière, *The Priest of the Eucharist*, (New York: Fathers of the Blessed Sacrament, 1936) p.14.

4   André Guitton, *Peter Julian Eymard, Apostle of the Eucharist*, Pauline Publishing, (Montreal 1992) p.24.

5   Norman Pelletier, *Tomorrow Will Be Too Late* (Cleveland: Emmanuel Publishing, 1992) p.135.

abandoned in his divine Sacrament, of warring against the capital heresy of the century, indifference; of melting the ice that is hardening all hearts, of preaching the Eucharist in and out of season."[1]

When the time came for him to finally leave his beloved Marist Order to found a new Eucharistic Congregation, he was derided and harshly criticised by friends and foes alike.[2] The inspiration to found the new community came on a day on which he had prolonged his silent thanksgiving after Communion.[3] Again we are reminded of how many graces which changed the world were given to the saints in that most sacred of moments just after Mass. How much grace is lost because of a lack of attentiveness to the Lord after Holy Communion. He received this inspiration just after a solemn celebration of the feast of Saint Joseph. The saint would go on to teach beautifully about how Saint Joseph is a model for Eucharistic adorers.[4] He himself would try to become a "Saint Joseph of the Eucharist." In other words, he would try to live in the same communion of life with Christ Eucharistic as Saint Joseph once enjoyed in Nazareth. The floor of the holy house of Nazareth was like the first outspread corporal, and so who better than Joseph to teach us reverence and love for the Real Presence of Jesus.[5]

Though Saint Eymard was threatened by scrupulous souls that he would lose his soul for "reneging" on his Marist vows in order to found another community, nothing could stop the saint from running the course marked out for him by heaven. He had received his Eucharistic love from Our Lady's hands and he was

1 Saint Peter-Julian Eymard, *Retreat Notes*. Translated by William LaVerdiere, (Saint Meinrad, Indiana: Abbey Press, 1969) p. 280.

2 *Ibid.,* p.98.

3 Guitton, André. *Peter Julian Eymard, Apostle of the Eucharist,* (Montreal: Pauline Publishing, 1992) p.91.

4 Saint Peter-Julian Eymard, *The Month of Saint Joseph* (Cleveland: Emmanuel Publishing, 1938).

5 *Ibid.,* p. 59.

confident that her motherly heart would understand if he left her Order to give her Son the glory he deserves. Not only would she understand, but he felt that she herself was guiding his steps in this direction. In later life he would affirm that there is no other way to a Eucharistic vocation, except through Mary.[6] With Our Lady's help, he was determined to help devote his life to bearing witness to the personal nature of Christ's Eucharistic presence. He would establish an Order, what he called the most beautiful Order in the Church, which would offer to Jesus a royal form of perpetual Eucharistic worship.

Jesus Christ is the Messiah, and thus he is our King. He is the King of all Kings. In the introduction to this book, we showed that Jesus renounced the earthly kingship that was being forced upon him when he preached on the Eucharist. As a result of that one sermon on the Bread of Life, he lost all those followers who were ready and willing to proclaim him King. He chose a Eucharistic Kingship over an earthly one. In the Eucharist, he now reigns as our King and thus we should treat him as our royal Sovereign. He should be allowed to govern our souls by means of his Eucharistic love. Saint Peter-Julian Eymard understood this clearly and dedicated his entire life to offering Jesus in the Blessed Sacrament a kingly form of worship. Eymard would provide Jesus with a King's court in which he would be surrounded day and night by consecrated souls on fire with love for him. The sanctuary would be adorned in royal fashion with a crown above the monstrance. The monstrance itself would be as majestic as possible, and elevated on high with the extravagant solemnity it deserves.

This royal court on earth would try to match the courts of heaven in the fervour of its adoration! He dreamed of a kind of holy rivalry with the angels and saints in heaven, where we all try to outdo each other in our displays of love for the same

6   Saint Peter-Julian Eymard, *Our Lady of the Blessed Sacrament*, (Cleveland: Emmanuel Publishing, 1938) p.108-111.

Christ whom they gaze upon face-to-face and we through the Eucharistic veil. Saint Eymard envisaged the arrival of a new Eucharistic era. For him the Sun of the Eucharist had not yet fully begun to shine with full force, but the Eucharistic times were approaching. He said that in the royal adoration of his magnificent new community he was only perceiving the first ray of this great Eucharistic sunrise, but what would it not be like later?[1]

The Apostle of the Eucharist held that adoration is essentially a dialogue of love with Jesus.[2] It is not a monologue. We speak to him, but we must also listen to him. We must learn to open our inmost selves to the Eucharistic voice of Jesus, that voice which speaks to us in the silence of our hearts. In this way, our adoration will bring us into deep union with the Will of the Lord. In order to sustain and prolong this dialogue of love we should meditate on the life and words of Jesus. It is helpful to bring the Scriptures with us, for Christ loves to speak to us through his holy Word. The same Jesus who walked the face of the earth two thousand years ago is now alive and present before us in the Eucharist. Through the Eucharist, the joy of the Incarnation is in some sense prolonged, as Christ continues to make his sacred humanity present in the world. Saint Eymard was convinced that through the Eucharist, Jesus continues to transmit to our souls the grace of the virtues that he exercised during his mortal life two thousand years ago.[3] So with the Bible in our hands and our minds filled with the Word of God, we should come before the living Lord in awe-filled adoration. Then he himself will draw us into union with his Sacred Heart. When we enter correctly into this dialogue of love, Jesus fills us with the gifts of the Holy

---

1   Norman Pelletier, *Tomorrow Will Be Too Late* (Cleveland: Emmanuel Publishing, 1992) p.69.

2   Saint Peter Julian Eymard, *The Real Presence* (Cleveland: Emmanuel Publishing, 1938) p.1

3   *Ibid.,* p.7.

Spirit and clothes us with his own Eucharistic virtues and merits.

At the time when Saint Peter-Julian was founding his religious order there existed other movements of perpetual Eucharistic Adoration in the Church, but often their sole purpose was to make reparation for the sins of the world. However, the Apostle of the Eucharist corrected and expanded their understanding and helped them to see that reparation is indeed necessary, but that it is only one of the four ends of adoration. In our Holy Hours, our prayer should contain those four dispositions which are present in the perfect prayer of Christ himself, and to which we are united through the Blessed Sacrament, namely, adoration, thanksgiving, reparation and intercession.

In our own days we have lost something of the idea of making reparation for sins, but today we might be in danger of reducing adoration to the sole dimension of intercession. Often, people spend almost all of their Holy Hour interceding for others and for their own needs, but this is only meant to be one dimension of our prayer. Even in human relationships it is not fitting to begin a conversation by asking for something. We must enter into the dialogue appropriately and then come to the moment of making a request. The way to enter into dialogue with God is through meditation and love. We must contemplate God's goodness, praising and thanking him for it before we make requests of him. Eymard advises us to begin every Holy Hour with an act of love for Christ. "If you begin with yourself, you will stop halfway. (...) Does not a child kiss his mother before obeying her? The only door to the heart is love."[4] It is possible to divide our Holy Hour up into different segments, within which we concentrate on one of the four dimensions of adoration in a special way. Whatever way we are led to spend our time with Christ, our adoration should have something of these four dimensions of the perfect prayer which Jesus unceasingly offers to the Father on behalf of sinful humanity.

4   *Ibid.,* p. 4

Blessed Dina Bélanger
Apostle of Eucharistic Intimacy

Blessed Dina Bélanger, born in Quebec at the end of the nineteenth century, sacrificed a brilliant career as a pianist in order to enter the Congregation of Jesus and Mary. From the beginning of her religious life, and once she had fully entrusted herself to Our Lady, she was taken into the deepest form of intimacy with the Eucharistic Lord. This Marian and Eucharistic spirituality which reached its perfection during her religious life had been with her in seed-form from childhood. Among her earliest memories were the first hymns she learned, one of entrustment to Our Lady and another of adoration of the Eucharistic Lamb.[1] Her first Holy Communion was a key moment of grace and shortly thereafter she began to intensely desire to follow the path of holiness.

As a teenager Dina set herself a strict routine of daily prayer and meditation, as well as weekly Confession. By the age of fourteen she had already consecrated her virginity to Jesus and by age sixteen she had offered her life entirely to him to console his heart and save souls.[2] She would do both in royal fashion. One of the experiences she had in Eucharistic Adoration, while still a novice in the Congregation of Jesus and Mary, sums up her life of Eucharistic intercession for us: "One first Friday of the month, when the Blessed Sacrament was exposed, I seemed to see, during my private adoration, a multitude of souls rushing to their eternal damnation. Some were on the brink of the abyss; they were about to fall. Jesus told me that I could save them by praying fervently for them and offering him small sacrifices out of love. I did this at once. Then I saw these same souls, won over by divine grace, abandoning the camp of the demon."[3]

1   Dina Bélanger, *The Autobiography of Dina Bélanger.* (Quebec: Atelier Rouge, 1995) p.43.
2   *Ibid.* p.182.
3   *Ibid.* p.183.

To study her life is to learn the power of intercession before the Eucharistic Lord. She learned that Jesus is infinitely merciful and desires to forgive even the greatest sinners, but also that our intercession and sacrifice for them are indispensable. She was told that her intercession was so powerful not only because of her deep faith, but above all because of her love. In the same way that Mary, who has nothing but love in her heart, has an irresistible power to move the heart of Jesus, so too, this great saint, formed in the school of Mary became capable of saving innumerable souls by her prayer. Jesus told her: "Through my divine Heart, your power is infinite; you have a great part to play in the salvation and sanctification of all souls both now and in the future."[4] Adoration and daily fidelity to Christ became her spiritual combat through which she waged war on the powers of hell which keep souls imprisoned in sin. Friday became her day of intercession where she would snatch souls from Satan. Wednesday was given to her by Christ as a day to intercede for priestly and religious vocations. She learned that so many vocations are being lost because people are afraid of renunciation and want to enjoy this earthly life in a selfish manner.[5]

Jesus calls certain souls to live in deep intimacy with him in the Blessed Sacrament. He called this a kind of "need of his heart."[6] He repeats for these souls what he did for John at the Last Supper as he allowed him to rest his head upon his heart and receive secrets that others could not know. To these souls he wishes to reveal the thoughts of his heart, but alas there are very few who give him the time and attention that are necessary to receive this grace. In order to receive it the soul must be pure and must become accustomed to thinking constantly of Christ. Blessed Dina was faithful to the grace and received an abundance of supernatural insights for her efforts. Jesus told Dina that through his mother he had granted her

---

4   *Ibid.* p.305.
5   *Ibid.* p. 303, 317.
6   *Ibid.* 293.

the grace to think continually of him as he was thinking continually of her.[1] He even went so far as to reveal to her what he described as his "Eucharistic thought", the thought which best describes what is in his heart, the thought to which we should unite our thought while in adoration. It is a thought which expresses his desire to unite souls to his Eucharistic Heart and is best summarised by the following words which he first spoke on Holy Thursday: "Father, may they be one in us, as you are in me and I am in you."[2] This thought lets us enter into the inner movement of the Eucharistic Heart of Jesus and shows us that it is one of intercession for Trinitarian unity on earth, brought about by the power of the Blessed Sacrament.

Our Eucharistic Lord revealed to Dina the great anguish that is caused to his heart by the lack of love and attentiveness of the hearts of priests and religious. He gives them his love in a particular way and if they are not sensitive to that gift, they break his heart most bitterly. Many refuse to enter into deep intimacy with Christ because they are afraid that they might have to give up their attachments. Once when she was trying to console him for the disrespect with which some treat him in the Eucharist, he said: "I am far more sensitive to the lukewarm love of souls consecrated to me than I am to the sinful sacrileges and desecrations committed against me by my enemies."[3] Jesus made known to her in a special way how saddened he was by the manner of life of many of his priests, simply because of their lack of love for him. She would often hear his sorrowful lament: "My priests, my priests…" They trust too much in human means and their own activity. The gift he has given his priests is so powerful that if a priest were to live in intimacy with Jesus, then a mere glance at

1 Dina Bélanger, *The Autobiography of Dina Bélanger.* (Quebec: Atelier Rouge, 1995) p, 282-292.
2 *Ibid.* p.293.
3 *Ibid.* p..269, 275, 349.

him on the street would be enough to raise a person's mind to the things of heaven. People would feel as though another Jesus Christ had just walked past them. He lamented that his priests were often learned and eloquent, but lacked the holiness which comes from an intense interior life and which brings its own kind of knowledge. She learned that the tender heart of Christ in the Blessed Sacrament is thirsting for love and virtually begging for love from human souls. Love is not loved! So desirous is he of our love that he told her he would have suffered infinitely more than he did in his Passion just to secure the love of one soul.[4]

Echoing what he had once asked of Saint Margaret-Mary, Christ also asked Dina to do a Holy Hour each Thursday evening to console his heart. In these times she would be privileged to taste the interior bitterness which was his in Gethsemane. Her desire to know the heart of her Beloved made her long to suffer his pains. Jesus would speak ever more clearly to her heart just after Communion; his voice being preceded by a deep sense of peace. During the course of these mystical dialogues, he revealed to her that the intensity of the desire in his loving Eucharistic heart is so strong that it would take his human life were that possible. His desire is to reign in us by love and to flood us with grace. The Hebrew style double repetition of the word "desire" in the words he addressed to his friends just before the Last Supper gives to the meditative mind an intimation of this truth. "With desire have I desired to eat this Passover with you." (Luke 22:15) He gave her the following invocations which correspond to the desire of his heart and told her to pray the second one on behalf of all souls, both present and future, since a soul united to him can even affect people of subsequent generations:

> *Eucharistic Heart of Jesus, may your kingdom come, through the Immaculate Heart of Mary...*

4   *Ibid.* p. 160, 166, 356, 294, 295.

Eucharistic Heart of Jesus, burning with love for us, inflame our hearts with love for you.[1]

By the end of her short life, Blessed Dina was having profound experiences of the Blessed Trinity and her soul could no longer be kept in this world for much longer. So deep was her union with Jesus that he would call her: "My little myself."[2] She became a kind of "additional humanity" for Christ.[3] In spite of the fact that she had a perpetual awareness of the indwelling of the Trinity in her soul, she became ever more attached to the Eucharistic presence of Christ in the tabernacle. Her soul would be paralysed by love whenever she came before the Blessed Sacrament and she would literally have to drag herself away from the chapel, grieving whenever she was kept far away from the Sacred Host.[4] Her soul ached with the longing to be near the Sacred Heart of her Bridegroom at all times. She was feeling ever more intensely what she had written about a few years earlier: "If only souls realised what Treasure is theirs in the divine Eucharist, tabernacles would have to be protected by unassailable ramparts; for under the influence of a holy and all-consuming hunger, they would go by themselves to feed on the Manna of the seraphim; night and day, churches would be overflowing with worshippers consumed with love for the august Prisoner."[5] On the 4th of September 1929, after having just announced that the Blessed Virgin Mary was coming to take her, Dina's Eucharistic soul left this world in peace in the thirty-third year of her mortal life.[6]

---

1   *Ibid.* p. 36.
2   Ibid. p. 282.
3   Ibid. p. 237.
4   Ibid. p. 266.
5   Ibid. p. 231.
6   Ibid. p. 364.

Archbishop Fulton Sheen
Apostle of the Power Hour

"For priests, to whom Christ our Redeemer entrusted the office of consecrating and dispensing the mystery of His Body and Blood, can assuredly make no better return for the honour which has been conferred upon them, than by promoting with all their might the glory of his Eucharist, and by inviting and drawing the hearts of men to the health-giving springs of this great Sacrament and Sacrifice, seconding hereby the longings of His most Sacred Heart."[7] These words of Pope Leo XIII were put into practice and lived to the full by the great Archbishop Fulton Sheen. Though not yet officially raised to the altars of the Church, the bishop is well on his way to beatification. In spite of the fact that he was one of the most famous men in America in the mid-twentieth century, as well as the pioneer of a new form of evangelisation for the entire Universal Church, Sheen was always quick to affirm that he drew all of the grace for his mission from the Most Blessed Sacrament. He once visited Ireland to give a retreat for bishops and priests, during the course of which the question of where he drew so much grace and wisdom for his mission arose. The saintly bishop acknowledged that he did have a special power given to him for evangelisation, but in the same breath he affirmed that the power was not his own, but came from the One who dwells in the tabernacle. His daily Holy Hour, to which he was faithful for over sixty years, became known as his "Power Hour." Since he had totally entrusted himself to Our Lady every day from his youth, she had formed his heart and taught him the great secret of holiness, the secret of Eucharistic Adoration.

Faced with the painful crisis in the priesthood in the 1970's Sheen became convinced that a daily Holy Hour was necessary for all priests if they were to have any hope of remaining faithful

7   Pope Leo XIII, *Mirae Caritatis*, §19

to their vocation.[1] He noticed that when priests got themselves into crises, it did not happen all of a sudden, in one instant, but rather gradually and beginning with small compromises. He said that the destruction of a priestly vocation often began with a failure to visit the Eucharistic Saviour, except "officially" when one "had" to celebrate Mass or conduct devotions. This manifests a certain coldness of heart towards Christ which will lead to serious vocational problems eventually. For Sheen, when a man of God falls it is because somewhere along the line he "who is a priest because of the Eucharist failed to be a Eucharistic priest."[2] He saw that the daily Holy Hour was what would prevent this priestly disintegration from occurring. All vocations, whether those of priests or lay people, can benefit from this advice.

Sheen explained why it was good to insist specifically upon an hour of daily adoration.[3] The reasons he provided are both biblical and psychological. The idea of the "hour" often occurs in the Gospels and it is almost always a reference to the Passion. As the Lord was handed over to his executioners he spoke of an hour of darkness which had arrived. (Luke 22:53) The hour refers to the moment in which the innocent One is handed over to the guilty, when sinners would have their way with the sinless body of Christ. In that hour of treachery and pain, the Lord turned and asked his best friends for the only favour he ever implored from them, that they might keep watch with him one hour. It was his wish that the hour of wickedness be met with an hour of love. The apostles were asked to give him an hour of consolation in reparation for the hour of darkness and to console his heart when all around was infidelity and evil.

---

1   Fulton Sheen, *The Priest Is Not His Own* (San Francisco: Ignatius Press, 2004) p. 243-255.

2   *Ibid.* p. 219.

3   Fulton Sheen, *Treasure in Clay* (New York: Image Books/Doubleday, 1980) p. 196-209.

Today we are living through a new hour of darkness. Whatever evil is done to the least of his brothers Christ considers as done to himself. It is his own innocence that is being attacked in the lives of the innocent unborn children who are slaughtered by the thousand every day. His own Mystical Body of the Church is being rent asunder by divisions and infidelity. His own sacred Eucharistic body is being treated like a dead object to be consumed by whosoever approaches it and demands the "right" to do so. In this new hour of darkness, Jesus again turns to his most faithful friends and begs them to watch one hour with him. His Sacred Heart, which he told Saint Margaret Mary thirsted for love in the Blessed Sacrament, cries out for love in the arid desert of the post-modern world. In a previous chapter we showed that by means of the Holy Sacrifice of the Mass Christ makes reparation to the Father for the sins of the world. In Eucharistic Adoration, we make reparation to the Son for all the ingratitude, indifference, and sacrileges which pierce his loving heart anew.

All over the world, faithful souls are hearing the silent plea from the tabernacle to keep watch one hour. Thus, the faithful are forming great chains of perpetual adoration and love to console their Eucharistic Friend. In spite of the great loss of Eucharistic faith, never before in the Church was there as much adoration as there is today. Thanks to all of this adoration there is hope for the Church and the world. The self-sacrificial love of those who respond to Christ's calling to watch one hour with him is surely stemming the tide of evil and preventing it from totally sweeping over the world. The daily damage done to the Church's mission by sacrilegious Communions is being repaired by all of the adoration. Through the love of Christ's faithful, power is slowly coming back into the Church and giving her the courage and grace to launch out upon a new evangelisation.

So, the first reason given by Sheen for doing a daily Holy Hour is rooted in a biblical mystery. It is a calling from Christ in the hour of darkness. The second reason is a psychological one. We live in the most anti-contemplative epoch in human history. Never before has there been a time in which there is so much noise, so many distractions, and immoral temptations hurled at us each day. Our ancestors knew nothing of this frenzy which we call daily life, and so the contemplative spirit came easier to them. We, for our part, need to spend more time in prayer than they did, not only in order to repair the interior disorders exacerbated by modern media, but also in order to be able to get ourselves into a meditative state in which contact with the presence of Christ will be possible. An hour of prayer provides sufficient time for this contemplative process to take place. For most of the first twenty or thirty minutes we will probably be simply detaching ourselves from the world and from the mental whirlwind of our distractions. Only after that will we be able to have a proper heart-to-heart dialogue with Christ.

In order to explain this psychological need to spend at least an hour in adoration, Fulton Sheen used the example of what happens in the Gospel on the road to Emmaus. The two men failed to recognise the Lord as they walked along the road, sad and dejected by the tragedy of his death. Eventually, as they journeyed onwards together, he began to correct their erroneous way of thinking. Then he started to explain the true meaning of the Word of God, causing their hearts to burn within them with holy desire. Finally, they were led to recognise his Holy Face in the "breaking of bread" before he vanished and they returned to Jerusalem to announce his resurrection. All of this can be used to describe what should ordinarily happen in a Holy Hour. First, we struggle to recognise the face of Jesus in the Host because we are too distracted. Additionally, we are often sad and discouraged by the trials of life. This sadness will be deeper in those who spend much time watching news and television. The spirit of the world is a spirit which brings sadness and a dampening of the fire of the

Holy Spirit within us. The world also causes us to think erroneously about reality, just as the two men were thinking about the errors being discussed by all of Jerusalem.

As we spend time in silence before the Eucharistic Lord, he slowly corrects our way of thinking. He then begins to sow in our hearts the seeds of hope for the future. From within us, good and holy thoughts begin to rise up and drive out the darkness in our hearts. Archbishop Fulton Sheen always recommended bringing the Gospel to adoration. As we meditate upon it in the presence of Christ, he himself guides us to understand it aright, and he communicates deeply to our hearts through his Word. When we perceive him speaking to us, our hearts begin to burn with holy desires, with inner movements of peace and hope. And then we raise our eyes to the monstrance and recognise that he is truly hidden there, that he is speaking to us; and since this is the case, we have nothing to fear. We rejoice in his presence and speak to him of the love and gratitude in our hearts. By the time we leave the chapel we are ready and eager to go back into the world and announce the Gospel to others, to let all people know that the Lord is risen and alive today in the Blessed Sacrament!

Saint Carlo Acutis
Eucharistic Apostle of the Internet

The canonisation of Saint Carlo Acutis in September 2025 was a cause of great joy for the Church. Young people all over the world can look to him for an example not only of heroic virtue but also of intense Eucharistic fervour. Born in London in 1991 and having spent most of his short life in Italy, he was seized by love of the Blessed Sacrament from a very young age. His use of the internet to make known his world-famous presentation of Eucharistic miracles bears witness to the spiritual profit that can be made of it by a virtuous soul, notwithstanding the destructive influence that it has had on the moral life of so many of his contemporaries. When an account of the Eucharistic miracles which fascinated him so much are presented to young people today, this often has a profound effect upon them. Perhaps this young saint has taught us a way in which we can effectively transmit faith in the Real Presence of Christ in the Blessed Sacrament to the youth of our times.

His own love for the Eucharist seems to have begun to take shape at an early age, under the influence of a Polish nanny who would take him for visits to the tabernacle. Grasping that the Eucharist is truly the body and blood of Christ, the little boy requested to make his first Holy Communion earlier than normal. Granted permission to receive the Lord at age seven, he made the following resolution on that unforgettable day: "to always be united with Jesus, that is my life's goal."[1] The special Eucharistic graces he received in that moment caused within him a desire to receive Holy Communion on a daily basis, as well as to spend time each day in silent awe before the Blessed Sacrament.

His experience illustrates the importance of doing all we can to help children to receive their first Holy Communion with profound reverence and love. Carlo's short prayer to Jesus during the moment of Communion is simple and yet powerful if said sincerely: "Jesus, come in! Make yourself at home!"[2] Christ comes in order to dwell in us forever and so as to take life in the world once again through us. If we truly want him to be at home in us, we will rid from our lives all that would make him feel unwelcome. So confident was Carlo in the power of attending daily Mass with the correct dispositions that he would boldly proclaim: "If we approach the Eucharist every day, we will go straight to heaven!"[3]

1   Antonia Salzano Acutis, *My Son Carlo: Carlo Acutis Through the Eyes of His Mother*, (Tasmania: Cana Press, 2025), p. 104.
2   *Ibid.* p. 216
3   *Ibid.*

The Eucharistic fervour of the young man of God ultimately rubbed off on his parents. His contagious childlike fire of zeal for the Eucharistic Lord could not but influence those closest to him. This is a familiar pattern which can be observed among many young Catholics of recent decades. In a reversal of classical roles, they are often the ones who help to deepen faith in the hearts of their parents. This was certainly the case in the life of Saint Carlo Acutis. His mother observed that the Eucharist had become the centre of the boy's life, remarking that "his creativity and constructive energy flowed outward from his daily Mass attendance."[4] Desiring to spread Eucharistic love to others and making use of the internet to do so he eventually created his famous website detailing many of the Eucharistic miracles which heaven has granted us down through the ages to strengthen weak faith.

The saint was also known for his active love for the poor and homeless. Perceiving Christ in the Eucharist he became capable of perceiving him truly present in those who suffer. Saint Teresa of Calcutta who also had a remarkable grace to see Jesus present in the poorest of the poor intimated that it was her contemplation of Christ in the Blessed Sacrament each morning which provided her with the gift of deeper spiritual vision. Beholding him hidden behind the appearances of the sacred Host we come to be able to look with greater reverence at the souls redeemed by his precious blood. At an early age, Saint Carlo learned this secret of sanctity. In preparing us for the Last Judgment, Christ insisted upon the need for charity towards those in need. If it was through the Eucharist that Carlo obtained this grace then it is not surprising that he called the Eucharist his highway to heaven. The church at his funeral was overflowing with friends, beggars, homeless people (...) all of whom he had helped during his short fifteen years of life. Not long after his death his famous exhibition of Eucharistic miracles would be travelling the globe to spread Eucharistic awe to parishes everywhere.

4   *Ibid.* p. 194

Saint Carlo was also aware of the indispensable role of the Most Blessed Virgin Mary in the life of all those who desire to love the Eucharistic Lord and to stay faithful to him in the struggles of life. Here was his advice for how we should pray during the Eucharistic Prayer of the Mass which mystically transports us to Calvary: "We have to ask for grace from God the Father through the merits of his only Son, Jesus Christ, his five holy wounds, his most Precious Blood, and the tears and sadness of the Virgin Mary, who as his mother, can intercede on our behalf more than anyone else."[1] In conclusion, we can say that to Catholics of today—and especially to our young people – Saint Carlo offers five simple but efficacious steps towards holiness: pray the most holy Rosary so as to make a daily entrustment of our lives to Our Lady, go to Confession regularly, to Mass daily, spend silent time in adoration before the Eucharistic Lord, and then learn to see him in the poor and in those most in need of our love.[2]

Saint Manuel Gonzalez
Apostle of the Abandoned Tabernacle

On October 16th, 2016, the Church canonised Saint Manuel Gonzalez, the bishop of the "Abandoned Tabernacle." Born in Seville, Spain, on February 25th, 1877, he developed a great love for Our Lady and the Eucharist as a child. As soon as he was ordained a priest he became a zealous promoter of Eucharistic Adoration as a result of a spiritual experience he had before an abandoned tabernacle. Shocked to see the dust and cobwebs with which it was surrounded, his heart was pierced by an immense sorrow for the outrage of how the second Person of the Blessed Trinity is treated by so many people. Jesus has given us everything

---

1   *Ibid.* p. 215

2   See Monsignor Anthony Figueiredo, *Blessed Carlo Acutis: 5 Steps to Being a Saint,* (London: Catholic Truth Society, 2021).

in giving us his very self in the Blessed Sacrament, yet we leave him abandoned in many churches day and night. Years later Saint Manuel would describe what happened when he looked at the Lord in his abandoned tabernacle on that day which changed his life forever and set him on the path to sainthood:

> *My faith was looking at Jesus through the door of that Tabernacle, so silent, so patient, so good, gazing right back at me… His gaze was telling me much and asking me for more. It was a gaze in which all the sadness of the Gospel was reflected; the sadness of "no room at the Inn", the sadness of those words: "Do you also want to leave Me?", the sadness of poor Lazarus begging for crumbs from the rich man's table, the sadness of the betrayal of Judas, the denial of Peter, of the soldier's slap, of the spittle in the Praetorium, and the abandonment of all. (…)*
>
> *The gaze of Jesus in that Tabernacle was a gaze that pierced the soul and one can never forget it. (…) All my illusions about the kind of priest I would be vanished. I found myself to be a priest in a town that didn't love Jesus, and I would have to love Him in the name of everybody in that town.*[3]

The abandoned tabernacle filled him with zeal to spend himself making Jesus in the Eucharist known and loved. The method he suggested for adoration was similar to that of Saint Peter-Julian Eymard, namely, to enter into a simple conversation with Christ based upon a mystery from the Gospel. He never tired of repeating that the Christ of the Gospel and the Christ of the tabernacle are one. If we want to know Jesus truly, we need both the Eucharist and meditation of the life of Christ. He spoke beautifully of the gift of the Gospel which we sometimes neglect: "Sometimes we lament the fact that photography wasn't invented

---

3   Saint Manuel Gonzalez. *D. Manuel Gonzalez, Obras Completas,* (Burgos, Spain: Editorial Monte Carmelo, 1998), Vol. 1, §15-18.

at the time of Jesus, so that we could have a picture of Him. What joy to be able to look at the picture and say: that was Him! Nevertheless, that picture would not have given us more joy than the Gospel gives us. A picture of Jesus, as beautiful and perfect as it would be, would always be merely a picture of Him from the outside and in only one attitude. The Gospel is the picture of Jesus from both within and without, and in different attitudes."[1]

We notice that so many of the Eucharistic saints insist upon using the Scriptures, and especially the Gospels, when we are in adoration. This kind of biblical adoration has a profound effect upon the soul, preparing it for eternal life. The faculties of the soul must be made ready to behold God in the beatific vision. The sinful human mind is not naturally disposed to gaze upon the blazing light of God's essence. The heart is not naturally ready to love him as he ought to be loved. Essentially, the beatific vision consists of the intellectual vision of the inner life of God, which results in the will coming to perfect rest in him. The intellect is prepared for this by pondering the Word of God, and the will is prepared by reaching out to Christ in love. As we hold the mysteries of Christ's life in our minds, we glimpse the highest revelation of the Godhead, and this stirs our wills to greater acts of love for the Lord. Both movements of mind and will should always happen during the Holy Hour. Adoration then becomes a miniature prefiguration of the moment when we will see God face-to-face. Concretely, we can slowly ponder the life of Christ until our hearts are moved. Once we are touched by his light we then pause and allow our souls to rest in his Eucharistic love. This type of prayer is a simple and delightful way to prepare ourselves for the fulfilment of every desire in heaven

In 1915, Saint Manuel became a bishop and went on to found several associations and religious orders to ensure that Jesus would always be surrounded by a fitting guard of honour and love in this

1   *Ibid.*, Vol. 1, §394.

world. This was his advice to certain priests who were discouraged by the failure of their efforts to evangelise: "Very often I hear questions coming from wounded priestly and apostolic hearts. These questions are: What can be done to turn those who are Christians merely by name into real Christians? How can we make them live their Christian faith and morals? What can be done to make them come back to a holy and fruitful Christian austerity? In a word, how can we convert this world which after twenty centuries of Christianity is obstinately going back to the most corrupt and degrading paganism? The answer to these heartfelt questions can be found in one word: Go to the Tabernacle! Priests, go to the Tabernacle! Let us draw power from the Tabernacle! Nobody goes to the Father except through His Son, Jesus. He is the Way, the Truth, and the Life! We do not journey along this Way, this Truth and Life of God merely by speculative, intellectual studies of Jesus, but by living faith in Him, by constant contact with Him in his present state on earth which is his sacramental state."[2]

He tried to make his entire diocese aware of the infinite spiritual power that is available to us always in the tabernacle, if only we would go there to unleash it by our adoration: "As the water in the stream gives off freshness and moisture, although nobody approaches its banks; or as the rose breathes forth perfume although nobody gets close enough to smell it, in the same way, the Heart of Jesus in the Tabernacle, abandoned and alone, is always exhaling power."[3] A fountain of peace flows out from the Eucharist at every moment, even if there is nobody present to receive this peace.

During a visit to Zaragoza in 1939, he fell seriously ill and was transferred to Madrid, where he passed away on January 4th, 1940.

2   Saint Manuel Gonzalez. *D. Manuel Gonzalez, Obras Completas,* (Burgos, Spain: Editorial Monte Carmelo, 1998), Address to the Priests.
3   Saint Manuel Gonzalez. *D. Manuel Gonzalez, Obras Completas,* (Burgos, Spain: Editorial Monte Carmelo, 1998), Vol. 1, §406.

Before he died, he wrote the following epitaph to be placed at his tomb: "I ask to be buried next to a Tabernacle, so that my bones, after death, as my tongue and my pen during life, can say to those who pass by: Jesus is there! There He is! Do not leave Him abandoned!"[1] Pope John Paul II spoke beautifully of Saint Manuel at the Eucharistic Congress in Seville in 1993. He said that this man of God was sent to show us that our response to the presence of Christ in the tabernacle is often inadequate.[2] The simple lesson that we learn from this saintly bishop's life is that we should all play our part in ensuring that no tabernacle near us will ever be left abandoned. Pope Francis, who canonised Saint Manuel in 2016, reiterated the simple message that had been the saint's life's work: "Moreover, I want to encourage everyone to visit – if possible, every day – especially amid life's difficulties, the Blessed Sacrament of the infinite love of Christ and His mercy, preserved in our churches, and often abandoned, to speak filially with Him, to listen to Him in silence, and to peacefully entrust yourself to Him."[3]

Saint John Paul II
Apostle of the New Eucharistic Evangelisation

Those who knew Pope John Paul II testify that he was a man completely governed and guided by prayer. All of his decisions came forth from deep prayerful discernment. People would have to accustom themselves to the fact that he would regularly drift off into silent prayer, even while in the presence of others. We are reminded of that scene from Sacred Scripture in which Jesus appears to be praying in deep silence while in the presence of

1   *Ibid.*, Vol. 1, Introduction.
2   Pope John-Paul II, Homily for the 45th International Eucharistic Congress, Seville, June 12, 1993
3   Pope Francis, Message to the National Eucharistic Congress in Genoa, 7 July 2016.

his friends (Luke 9:18). The pope's entire life became a prayer. His missionary activity was always preceded by extended periods in Eucharistic Adoration. From his earliest years as a priest, he would spend long hours prostrate in adoration before the tabernacle, not fearing to manifest with external signs his interior amazement before the Eucharistic presence. Sometimes he would do this throughout the entire night. His spirit of recollection just before and after Mass was palpable, and those priests who concelebrated with him could see that this was not the time for conversation. He wrote many of his great works and homilies while in contemplation before the tabernacle, drawing inspiration from the Eucharistic Lord. He said: "What a privilege to be able to live and work in the shadow of His Presence, such a powerfully magnetic Presence!"[4]

Pope John Paul II also spoke of the joy of having a chapel in his own home, as well as the responsibility it brings of being attentive to the Lord: "Every bishop enjoys the privilege of maintaining a chapel in his own home, so close that he can reach out and touch it, but this privilege also brings with it great responsibility. The reason for having a chapel so close is so that everything in the bishop's life—his teaching, his decisions, his pastoral care—might begin from the feet of Christ, concealed in the Blessed Sacrament."[5] This is a great example for those of us who are priests and for all those who teach and work for the Church. The Eucharistic Lord should be able to personally govern and guide his Church through us; and he will, if we are attentive to his silent voice in the tabernacle. If we prepare our teachings before the Blessed Sacrament there is also less chance of us getting ourselves into trouble! The saintly John Paul once famously went so far as to say that the Eucharistic Jesus was the real owner of

4 Pope John Paul II, Rise, *Let Us Be On Our Way* (New York: Warner Books, 2004) p.147.
5 *Ibid.* p.145-146

his episcopal residence, while he himself was just the short-term tenant.[1] This may sound like a merely pious statement, but it is really an important truth. The Church exists for Jesus in the Blessed Sacrament. He is truly the Lord of the entire house of the Church. No matter what position we may find ourselves occupying, we are only ever at the service of Jesus Eucharistic. He must increase and we must decrease!

Pope John Paul II once said: "To evangelise the world there is need of apostles who are "experts" in the celebration, adoration and contemplation of the Eucharist."[2] Saint John Paul was himself an apostle because he was a Eucharistic "expert." Today the Church needs many souls like him, ready to enter into the inner sanctuary of the Eucharistic Heart of Jesus and to draw from that infinite source of divine grace the power to go out and pierce the darkness of our world with a proclamation of the luminous truth of the Gospel. Only in and through the Eucharistic mystery will we find the light that will transfigure us and the fire that will consume us to such a degree that we will once again become unstoppable apostles of Jesus Christ. In the third chapter of the Gospel of Saint Mark we read that the apostles were those men who were called to be with Jesus and to be sent out preaching. (Mk. 3:14) Nothing has changed. Through the Eucharist, the apostolic experience of Galilee has come to us. We are called to spend time with the same Christ, and when our souls have been flooded with his peace and grace, to go out and make him known in the world. To make Christ known we must first truly know him; and in order to know him, we must spend time in the light of his Real Presence, meditating on his holy Word.

With this truth in mind, Pope John Paul II also said during the Eucharistic Congress in Seville:

1 *Ibid.* p. 147
2 Pope John Paul II—Message for World Mission Sunday, April 19, 2004.

Join me in asking Jesus Christ the Lord, who died for our sins and rose for our salvation, that after this Eucharistic Congress the whole Church may be strengthened for the New Evangelisation which the entire world needs: new, also because of its explicit and deep reference to the Eucharist as the centre and root of Christian life, as the seed and requisite of fellowship, justice, and service to all men, starting with those who are most needy in body and in spirit. Evangelisation through the Eucharist, in the Eucharist, and from the Eucharist: these are three inseparable aspects of how the Church lives the mystery of Christ and fulfils her own mission of communicating him to all people.[3]

We evangelise *through* the Eucharist, praying for those to whom we will announce the Gospel, and having as our ultimate goal their encounter with the Eucharistic Lord. When we adore, it is Jesus himself who begins to evangelise and touch souls by his divine power. We evangelise *in* the Eucharist, by celebrating Mass so beautifully that souls will know that it is a true encounter with Almighty God. The irreverent "rushed Masses" which have become so common today are slowly eroding the faith of many, and preventing others from encountering Jesus in the Eucharist. They work contrary to evangelisation and we must pray that they come to an end as soon as possible. We evangelise *from* the Eucharist, by drawing all of our strength from adoration, and

---

3   *Chiedete con me a Gesù Cristo, il Signore, morto per i nostri peccati e risorto per la nostra salvezza, che, dopo questo Congresso Eucaristico, tutta la Chiesa esca rafforzata per la nuova evangelizzazione di cui il mondo intero ha bisogno: nuova, anche per il riferimento esplicito e profondo all'Eucaristia, come centro e radice della vita cristiana, come semina ed esigenza di fratellanza, di giustizia, di servizio a tutti gli uomini, a partire dai più bisognosi nel corpo e nello spirito. Evangelizzazione per l'Eucaristia, nell'Eucaristia e dall'Eucaristia: sono tre aspetti inseparabili di come la Chiesa vive il mistero di Cristo e compie la propria missione di comunicarlo a tutti gli uomini.* (Pope John-Paul II, Homily for the 45th International Eucharistic Congress, Seville, June 12, 1993, Author's translation.)

by becoming so like Christ that we will naturally lead souls to heaven. We become like those with whom we spend much time!

Pope John Paul makes clear that the New Evangelisation will be a fruit of Eucharistic love, having as its ultimate goal the drawing of all people to the feet of the Eucharistic Lord. It is insufficient to merely lead souls to make an act of faith in Jesus their Lord and Saviour. This is only the beginning of the spiritual life and the path to sanctity, but as we know, this little fire will need to be fanned into a strong and steady flame over the years. For this to happen, souls must discover the hidden presence of the Word Incarnate in the Eucharist. Only when this treasure of all treasures has been discovered will the soul be set on the straight path to holiness and eternal life. People who become adorers soon become faithful and constant friends of Jesus Christ, while others often fall away. The demands of the Christian life become an easy yoke and a light burden, once Jesus gives us his own strength, through the daily Eucharist encounter. So, we must lead the souls whom we evangelise, little by little, to recognise the Holy Face of Jesus, hidden behind the Eucharistic veil.

It was Saint John Paul's deep holiness and interior union with the Will of God that made him such a powerful witness of Jesus Christ. With great fervour, he travelled to the ends of the earth as an indomitable fisher of men. His witness drew multitudes back to the House of the Father. After a single encounter with him, many young people gave themselves over to living out the demands of the Christian life. Young men whose hearts were divided would at last respond to their priestly calling after merely glimpsing the saintly pope.

What was the secret of his holiness? It was rooted in a deep spiritual life which itself was supported by two unshakeable pillars. The first was his well-known devotion to the Most Blessed Virgin Mary. "*Totus Tuus*" were the words of filial love he addressed to the heart of his heavenly mother each day, thereby renewing his act of total consecration to her. He once said that discovering the masterpiece of the *True Devotion to Mary* written by St. Louis de Montfort was a turning-point in his life. It raised him to a new spiritual plane and became for him the short, straight, and easy path to union with Christ. From that moment forth he would make of his entire existence a pure gift of love to Jesus through Mary. He became a priest of the heart of Mary, formed in that blazing furnace of love in which she plunges those souls who abandon themselves to her, in imitation of the Incarnate Word who as a Child depended upon her for everything.

The second pillar of his spiritual life was the intense love for the Eucharist to which Our Lady led him. A study of Saint John Paul's life reveals how deeply devoted to Eucharistic Adoration he was: "To live the Eucharist it is necessary, as well, to spend much time in adoration in front of the Blessed Sacrament, something which I myself experience every day drawing from it strength, consolation and assistance."[1] He was speaking from experience as one who knew how to pass from adoration to evangelisation. He learned the Eucharistic secret which made of him an extraordinary herald of the Gospel who drew souls to Jesus wherever he set his foot.

The renowned French journalist, André Frossard, who himself had a miraculous conversion before the Eucharist exposed, tells us how he felt when he first saw Pope John Paul II in St. Peter's Square. He writes:

> *We had learnt that he was from Poland. My impression was rather that he had left his nets on the shore of a lake and that he came straight from Galilee. I had never felt so close to the Gospel. (…) There was no room for doubt. The astonished crowd in the square, lifting their faces to a new light, my neighbours, who were weeping, and I myself all shared the same feeling: Christianity was going to start again… it was*

1 Pope John Paul II, Message for World Mission Sunday, 19, April, 2004.

emerging once more from the tomb that everyone had thought finally sealed. This Pope would be the Pope of a Christian renewal, and with him the hope that had fled would return in strength among us.[1]

The holiness which provoked such a reaction of hope in the hearts of so many is the reason why Saint John Paul II's life contains the blueprint for the New Evangelisation. Holiness alone will draw this darkened, despairing world back to Christ. If we are to bring lost sheep back to the Good Shepherd, we too should imitate Pope John Paul II by consecrating ourselves to Our Lady and by allowing ourselves to be transfigured by the light which shines from the Eucharistic Face of Jesus. This is the path to apostleship today.

In the great Jubilee Year 2000, the pontiff returned to the Cenacle in Jerusalem to celebrate the Eucharist in the very place in which it had been instituted, and from which went forth the first evangelisation of the world. He was deeply touched by the experience of returning to the very source of Eucharistic grace. As the effects of the first evangelisation of the world were drawing to a close with the demise of Christendom, the Holy Father was tirelessly proclaiming the need for the Church to launch out upon a second evangelisation of the world. The offering of the Eucharist in the Cenacle by a saintly pope is another reminder that this must be a specifically Eucharistic evangelisation.

---

1   André Frossard, *Be Not Afraid* (New York: St. Martin's Press, 1982) p.8

VI

MARY—WOMAN OF THE EUCHARIST

Why was the Blessed Virgin Mary entrusted to Saint John at the foot of the Cross? If it were just a question of her now needing somebody to take care of her material needs, surely she could have been entrusted to some of the holy women instead. Were not those women already capable of taking care of the needs of Christ and the whole apostolic band? (Luke 8:3) Joanna was the very wife of Chuza, Herod's steward and one of the wealthiest men in Galilee. Our Lady's relative, Mary of Clopas, was herself present and would have gladly taken the sweet mother of Christ to live with her. No, if she was entrusted to John it was for another reason. It was not so that her material needs would be taken care of but rather her spiritual.[2] This was at least part of the reason for her mysterious entrustment to John. She needed the Blessed

2   Mother Maria Francesca Perillo, "Mary Coredemptrix and the Eucharist", *Mary at the Foot of the Cross VI* (New Bedford: Academy of the Immaculate, 2007), p. 239.

153

Sacrament to ease the agony of her exile here below, and so she needed the daily assistance of a priest. If the pope once granted Saint Catherine of Siena the daily services of a priest that she might have the Eucharist near her at all times, would not Our Lord do just as much for his own mother? In the company of Saint John, the Woman of the Eucharist would again be consoled by the Real Presence of that sacred body which was formed within her womb so many years before.

Mary and the Sacrifice-Sacrament

Even more than Mary's own need to be near her Eucharistic Son, we might also speak of her Son's "need" to have her near his Eucharistic mystery. The offering of the Holy Sacrifice of the Mass always makes present the infinite merits of Christ, but as we have shown in an earlier chapter, the measure of those merits which flow into the world at any given time depend upon the receptivity of those who assist at the Mass, as well as the general holiness of the Church in the moment that the Mass is offered. According to Cardinal Charles Journet, during Mary's mortal life, her presence single-handedly raised the entire level of the Church's charity to its highest plane. In speaking of how the efficacy of the Mass can rise and fall in different moments of the life of the Church he says: "It never has been so high as in the days of the newborn Church, when the Blessed Virgin assisted at the Mass of the Apostles, lifting up their offering by the force of her desire."[1] One Mass at which she prayed and offered herself while still clothed in mortal flesh was enough to flood the whole Church with grace. One movement of love in her pure heart was worth more to the Eucharistic Lord than the love of the entire angelic cohort.

---

1   Charles Journet *The Mass, the Presence of the Sacrifice of the Cross.* Translated by Victor Szczurek (South Bend Indiana: St. Augustine's Press, 2008) p. 123.

Our Lady was intimately associated with the offering of Christ on the hill of Calvary and she is still intimately associated with its re-presentation today. Mary's role in the mystery of Christ's sacrifice continues until the end of time in its Eucharistic mode of offering. Sister Lucy, the visionary of Fatima, saw this truth in the form of a vision. She said:

> *I had sought and obtained permission from my superiors and confessor to make a Holy Hour from eleven o'clock until midnight, every Thursday to Friday night. Being alone one night, I knelt near the altar rails in the middle of the chapel and, prostrate, I prayed the prayers of the Angel. Feeling tired, I then stood up and continued to pray the prayers with my arms in the form of a Cross. The only light was that of the sanctuary lamp. Suddenly the whole chapel was illuminated by a supernatural light, and above the altar appeared a cross of light, reaching to the ceiling. In a brighter light on the upper part of the cross, could be seen the face of a man and his body as far as the waist; upon his breast was a dove of light; nailed to the cross was the body of another man. A little below the waist, I could see a chalice and a large host suspended in the air, on to which drops of blood were falling from the face of Jesus Crucified and the wound in His side. These drops ran down onto the host and fell into the chalice. Beneath the right arm of the cross was Our Lady and in her hand was her Immaculate Heart. (It was Our Lady of Fatima, with her Immaculate Heart in her left hand, without sword or roses, but with a crown of thorns and flames.) Under the left arm of the cross, large letters, as if of crystal clear water which ran down upon the altar, formed the words: 'Grace and Mercy'.*[2]

The world is washed clean and irrigated with divine grace by the power of the Holy Sacrifice of the Mass. The graces of the

---

2   Andrew Apostoli, *Fatima For Today* (San Francisco: Ignatius Press, 2010) p.161.

Holy Sacrifice still flow down into the world in union with Mary, and so, in order to unite ourselves to the offering of Christ we should approach it through Mary. At the Mass, the sorrows and sacrifices of the members of the Church of all ages are joined to the sacrifice of Christ for the salvation of the world. Since Mary was the first to be taken into such a mystery, first on Calvary and then during her own mortal life through the Eucharist, she is the one through whom we can worthily enter into it in our own days. The extraordinary mystic and victim soul, Saint Veronica Giuliani, experienced this clearly: "While the priest consecrated the Most Divine Sacrament, as it was elevated on high, Mary Most Holy had me make that offering of myself, which I have always made in union with Jesus' offering for all on the Altar of the Cross. She made it with me and for me..."[1]

By the power of the Holy Sacrifice, what happened in Mary on Calvary is meant to happen in us in some small way at the Mass, namely, that Jesus might offer himself and us to the Father.[2] He makes of us an eternal offering to the Father, as it is put in the third Eucharistic Prayer. He is so one with us through grace that our sufferings are his sufferings, and he offers them to his Father as though they were his own. Before we approach the altar of God, we should always entrust ourselves to Our Lady, beseeching her to cultivate in us the correct Eucharistic dispositions. Experience teaches us that if we pray the Rosary before Mass, or even just part of it, if we are pressed for time, we will be able to retain our recollection and enter more deeply into the sacred mysteries.

---

1   Mother Maria Francesca Perillo, "Mary Coredemptrix and the Eucharist", *Mary at the Foot of the Cross VI* (New Bedford: Academy of the Immaculate, 2007), p. 260.
2   Dina Bélanger, *The Autobiography of Dina Bélanger* (Quebec: Atelier Rouge, 1995) p,314.

Mary and the Communion-Sacrament

The time we spend in thanksgiving after Holy Communion is supremely efficacious for bringing us into deeper intimacy with Christ. Although it would seem like the obvious time to remain recollected, it is very often the time when people are most distracted. It is a great victory for the enemy to have made so many people lose out on this key moment of grace in their spiritual lives. Archbishop Fulton Sheen once famously said that when a priestly vocation is ruined, it does not usually begin with some great act of infidelity, but rather with an apparently small one. He said it normally begins with a "fifteen-minute Mass" or a "one-minute thanksgiving."[3] What would the saintly archbishop not say today when we have reached the point where we would almost be content if we could convince people to make even a one-minute thanksgiving?

Yet, those souls who are consecrated to Mary, and who try to renew and live their consecration daily, seem to naturally fall into the habit of making a thanksgiving after Holy Communion. This deepened love for the gift of Holy Communion seems to be the common denominator in all those who live the true devotion to Mary. The Marian spirituality transcends all cultural and national boundaries, putting into souls an attentive love for the Eucharistic Person of Christ. The connection between devotion to Mary and love for the Eucharist is not surprising. She is the one who first welcomed Christ into the world. Her body was the first tabernacle, the first place of perpetual adoration. The Incarnation was like humanity's first Holy Communion, and thanks to Mary, the Eternal Word found a perfect welcome awaiting him. This is her role: to welcome Christ and to make him welcomed.

Certain saints teach us that we can ask Mary to welcome Jesus

3   Fulton Sheen, *The Priest Is Not His Own* (San Francisco: Ignatius Press, 2004) p. 219.

with us in the moment of Holy Communion. Saint Louis-Marie de Montfort spoke of this as the culmination of living the spirituality of total consecration to Mary:

> *Beg her to lend you her heart, saying, 'O Mary, I take you for my all; give me your heart." (…) After Holy Communion, close your eyes and recollect yourself. Then usher Jesus into the heart of Mary: you are giving him to his Mother who will receive him with great love and give him the place of honour, adore him profoundly, show him perfect love, embrace him intimately in spirit and in truth, and perform many offices for him of which we, in our ignorance, would know nothing. (…) The more you let Mary act in your Communion the more Jesus will be glorified.*[1]

The reception of Jesus with Mary in Holy Communion is probably the reason why Saint Louis-Marie de Montfort himself would eventually come to spend one full hour in thanksgiving after Communion.[2]

Saint Maximilian Kolbe also understood this grace and he said that when souls learn to live this kind of most radical form of consecration to Mary, then the Church will be raised to a new degree of love for Christ. He explained it in a conference he gave on March 28, 1937: "We are called to become like God; and to help us do so we have the Most Blessed Sacrament. How can we dispose ourselves so as to receive the greatest possible influx of grace? Let us consecrate ourselves to the Immaculata. Let her prepare us herself."[3] We can allow her to welcome Christ for us and with us in Holy Communion. The gentle meditation of one

1 Saint Louis-Marie de Montfort. *True Devotion to Mary.* no. 266, 270, 271.
2 Robert Fastiggi, "Mary and the Eucharist in Saint Louis de Montfort", *Mary at the Foot of the Cross VI* (New Bedford: Academy of the Immaculate, 2007), p. 292.
3 H.M. Manteau-Bonamy, *Immaculate Conception and the Holy Spirit* (Illinois: Marytown Press, 2008) p.106.

line of her *Magnificat* might be a good accompaniment to the attentive awareness of Christ's Real Presence within us. When we recall that the name of Jesus means "Saviour" the following line takes on a new meaning: "My spirit rejoices in God my Saviour." Blessed Dina Bélanger also discovered this secret of how to receive Communion with Mary, and at times she would even hear Our Lady speak to Jesus on her behalf during her thanksgiving after Communion.[4] She knew that the way to please Jesus is to "let Mary have her way in us."[5]

Mary and the Presence-Sacrament

The Blessed Virgin Mary is present wherever the Blessed Sacrament is present. She is there to form us in adoration and love for Christ. "At your right hand stands the queen in gold of Ophir" (Psalms 45:9). She herself adored him for decades in Nazareth. Every hour in the holy house of Nazareth was a Holy Hour. Mary and Joseph lived in an unceasing contemplation of the Eternal Word whom they called "Son." Not only did they live in adoration and contemplation, but also in a kind of holy familiarity with Jesus which is renewed and prolonged for us in every one of our adoration chapels. We live the life of Nazareth from the moment we begin to live in communion with Jesus in the monstrance. What a beautiful life is ours! Mary would return from fetching water at the well of Nazareth and feel an ecstatic surge of love rise up in her heart as she glimpsed the face of the Christ Child conversing with Joseph. The adorer who finishes a hard day's work in the weary world and who then makes his way to the adoration chapel for a visit knows this same thrill of love.

The witness of the Eucharistic saints also makes clear that the

4   Dina Bélanger, *The Autobiography of Dina Bélanger* (Quebec: Atelier Rouge, 1995) p.141.
5   *Ibid.* p.171

grace of Eucharistic Adoration is received through the Immaculate Heart of Mary. It is her work. Before we enter a chapel, we should always unite our souls to the soul of Mary, that she might love Christ with us and for us. Some people object: "But I want to focus on Christ alone." When we turn to Mary, we do not turn away from Christ, but rather turn more fully towards him. If we live in union with Mary we will come to love and please Jesus in a way that we could never have done without her. She loves him more intensely than the Seraphim; for none of them gave birth to their God. If we let her, she will share this love with us! In speaking of those who live the perfect consecration to Mary, St. Maximilian Kolbe said:

> *For just as the Immaculata herself belongs to Jesus and to God, so too, every soul through her and in her will belong to Jesus and to God in a much more perfect way than would have been possible without her. Such souls will come to love the Sacred Heart of Jesus much better than they have ever done up to now. Like Mary herself, they will come to penetrate into the very depths of love, to understand the Cross, the Eucharist, much better than before.*[1]

Blessed Dina Bélanger, who saw in a vision the connection between the Blessed Virgin Mary and the Eucharistic graces that we receive, offers us a fitting conclusion to these reflections with her "*Memorarae* to Our Lady of the Eucharistic Heart:"[2]

> Remember, Our Lady of the Eucharistic Heart,
> the unlimited power which Jesus has given you over His Heart
> in the Sacrament of His Love.

1   H.M. Manteau-Bonamy, *Immaculate Conception and the Holy Spirit* (Illinois: Marytown Press, 2008) p.115.

2   Dina Bélanger, *The Autobiography of Dina Bélanger* (Quebec: Atelier Rouge, 1995) p. 342.

Remember that you possess all His infinite riches
and that your divine Son always fulfils your requests
and your desires…

Reveal to the world the streams of peace and charity
which spring from the altar.

Our Lady of the Eucharistic Heart, admit us to the
court of the King of Love.

Be our model there until you welcome us into His
eternal court. Amen.[3]

3   Irène Léger, *Courage to Love* (Suffolk, UK: East Anglian Magazine Ltd.,
    1986) p. 146.

CONCLUSION

We will never fully understand while still on earth the intensity of the divine love that is at the origin of the mystery of the Eucharist. St Catherine of Siena who lived in such a profound union of heart with Christ was left stupefied by her experience of his love. She went so far as to say that it seemed to her that the Lord had been almost driven mad with love for souls. Only this love to the point of madness could explain to her why he would not only become a child for our salvation and end his life on the Cross, but also remain forever with us as our food.[1] It has been the aim of this book to at least begin to scratch the surface of this Eucharistic love. "If the love of Jesus in the Most Holy Sacrament does not win our hearts, Jesus is vanquished! Our ingratitude is greater than His goodness; our malice is more powerful than His charity!"[2]

Thankfully, it appears that we are beginning to witness a revival of Eucharistic love at this time. The first flowers of the

1   See St Catherine of Siena, *The Dialogue of St. Catherine of Siena*, (Charlotte: TAN Books, 2010) pp. 34,44.
2   Saint Peter Julian Eymard, *The Real Presence* (Cleveland: Emmanuel Publishing, 1938), p. 31.

Eucharistic springtime continue to bloom all over the globe. Day by day, the numbers of souls who discover the wonder of the Eucharist and feel themselves drawn to the holy Catholic Church is multiplying. In recent years, the number of young people converting to Catholicism has grown at a rate which few would have predicted. It is the Real Presence of Christ that is attracting them. The adorers who have been interceding before him for decades can be sure that their fidelity to adoration has been instrumental in obtaining the graces which are flowing into souls at this time. The Eucharist is the power source of divine grace ever present in our midst, and as long as there are adorers unleashing that power by means of their prayer, there is great hope for the renewal of the Church.

However, in order for the Church to be truly strong enough to evangelise the entire world, there is still much hard work needed with regard to the re-evangelisation of baptised Catholics. If the faithful come to understand the full truth about the Most Holy Eucharist—and the one who dwells with us day and night in the tabernacle—then the entire Church will receive a new outpouring of grace. The sad situation of parishes with no true Eucharistic devotion must come to an end. "Where the Eucharist is neglected, the Church has none but unfaithful children, and she will soon have to deplore fresh ruins."[1]

Zealous Eucharistic souls, willing to share the treasure they have discovered with their fellow Catholics in the pews, will greatly contribute to the strengthening of the interior of the Church, enabling her to recover her full missionary power to convert the world. Catholics whose experience of faith has consisted of little more than a shallow sacramentalisation with no depth of catechesis need to be brought into a living relationship with the Eucharistic Lord.

---

1   Saint Peter Julian Eymard, *The Real Presence* (Cleveland: Emmanuel Publishing, 1938), p.88.

Key to awakening Eucharistic faith and reverence is the role of Our Lady. Wherever the Rosary is prayed daily and Mary is loved, the Blessed Sacrament is also loved. In parishes in which Our Lady is honoured in a particular way—and especially in those that have been consecrated to her—the Eucharist is treated with reverence. One of the high-points of the entire ministry of Saint Jean-Marie Vianney—who was immensely fruitful in the apostolate—was the solemn consecration of his parish to the Immaculate Heart of Mary. The more that devotion to the Blessed Virgin Mary spreads in the Church, the more "Eucharistic Amazement" will deepen, and souls will learn to live from the three glorious dimensions of the Sacrament of Love as a mystery of communion, sacrifice, and perpetual presence. If we want to bring people to the Eucharistic Christ then we should do so always dependent upon the help of Our Lady.

It seems fitting to allow some words from the Apostle of the Eucharist, St Peter-Julian Eymard, to bring this work to a close. He foresaw the arrival of a new era of Eucharistic devotion and he issued a battle cry to bear witness boldly to the Real Presence of Christ, so that Jesus will take up his reign of love in souls. He said: "The Apostles could not show the Eucharist as we can. It even had to be hidden in those days on account of the persecutions. Its time had not yet come. It was necessary to conquer the world by the Cross of Jesus Christ before raising a throne for him to reign on. But today he wants to manifest himself; he wants to reign everywhere: this is the Age of the Blessed Sacrament which is dawning. Ask for the expansion of the reign of Jesus Christ in the Blessed Sacrament; pray to him to create servants and apostles for his reign of love, so that he may very soon be known, loved, and served by everyone. "Thy Kingdom come!"[2]

2 Saint Peter-Julian Eymard, *The Eucharist and Christian Perfection II.* (New York: Sentinel Press, 1948) p.125.

Bibliography

Antier, Jean-Jacques. *Charles de Foucauld*. Translated by Julia Shirek Smith. San Francisco: Ignatius Press, 1999.

Bélanger, Dina. *The Autobiography of Dina Bélanger*. Quebec: Atelier Rouge, 1995.

Beale, Gregory K. *The Temple and the Church's Mission*. Leicester: Apollos Publishing, 2004.

Cantalamessa, Raniero. *Words of Light: Inspiration from the Letters of Padre Pio*. Massachusetts: Paraclete Press, 2008.

Concannon, Thomas. *At the Court of the Eucharistic King*. Dublin: Gill and Son Co., 1929.

Convert, Abbé H. *The Curé of Ars and the Holy Eucharist*. Minnesota: The Neumann Press, 2000.

Crean, Thomas. *The Mass and the Saints*. San Francisco: Ignatius Press, 2008.

Da Riese, Fernando. *Padre Pio da Pietrelcina: Crocifisso senza Croce*. San Giovanni Rotondo: Edizioni Padre Pio, 1975.

De Goesbriand, Louis. *Catholic Memoirs of Vermont and New Hampshire*. Burlington: Press of R. S. Styles, 1886.

Faber, Frederick. *The Blessed Sacrament*. Rockford, Illinois: Tan

Books, 1978.

Frossard, André. *Be Not Afraid*. New York: St. Martin's Press, 1982.

Guitton, André. *Peter Julian Eymard, Apostle of the Eucharist*. Montreal: Pauline Publishing, 1992.

Hahn, Scott. *Consuming the Word*. New York: Image, 2013.

Journet, Charles. *The Mass, the Presence of the Sacrifice of the Cross*. Translated by Victor Szczurek. South Bend, Indiana: St. Augustine's Press, 2008.

————. *Le Mystère de l'Eucharistie*. Paris: Téqui, 1980.

Manelli, Stefano. *Jesus: Our Eucharistic Love*. New Bedford: Academy of the Immaculate, 2014.

Maritain, Jacques. *The Peasant of the Garonne*. New York: Holt, Rinehart and Winston Publishing, 1968.

Morrow, Thomas. *The Glory of the Mass*. Homiletic and Pastoral Review.

Nayar, Sheila. *Dante's Sacred Poem*. London: Bloomsbury, 2014.

O'Connor, James. *The Hidden Manna*. San Francisco: Ignatius Press, 1988.

Pelletier, Norman. *Tomorrow Will Be Too Late*. Cleveland: Emmanuel Publishing, 1992.

Perillo, Mother Maria Francesca. "Mary Coredemptrix and the Eucharist." In *Mary at the Foot of the Cross VI*. New Bedford: Academy of the Immaculate, 2007.

Pitre, Brant. *Jesus and the Jewish Roots of the Eucharist*. New York: Doubleday, 2011.

————. *Jesus and the Last Supper*. Grand Rapids: Eerdmans, 2015.

Rutler, George. *The Curé d'Ars Today*. San Francisco: Ignatius Press, 1998.

Antonia, Salzano Acutis. *My Son Carlo: Carlo Acutis Through the Eyes of His Mother*, Tasmania: Cana Press, 2025.

St Catherine of Siena. *The Dialogue of St. Catherine of Siena*, Charlotte: TAN Books, 2010.

Saint Francis de Sales. *Introduction to the Devout Life*. New York:

Dover Publications Inc., 2009.

Saint Leonard of Port Maurice. *The Hidden Treasure: Holy Mass.* Charlotte: Tan Books, 2012.

Saint Peter-Julian Eymard. *The Real Presence.* Ohio: Emmanuel Publishing, 1938.

———. *Our Lady of the Blessed Sacrament.* Cleveland, Ohio: Emmanuel Publishing, 1938.

———. *Retreat Notes.* Translated by William LaVerdiere. Saint Meinrad, Indiana: Abbey Press, 1969.

———. *The Month of Saint Joseph.* Cleveland, Ohio: Emmanuel Publishing, 1938.

Saint Teresa of Avila. *The Way of Perfection.* Translated and edited by E. Alison Peers. New York: Image Books, 1964.

Saint Therese of Lisieux. *The Story of a Soul.* Translated by John Beevers. New York: Doubleday, 1989.

Tesnière, Albert. *The Priest of the Eucharist.* New York: Fathers of the Blessed Sacrament, 1936.

Tolkien, J.R.R. *The Silmarillion.* New York: Houghton Mifflin Company, 2004.

The Good Shepherd Sisters. *The Life of Little Nellie of Holy God.* Charlotte: TAN Books, 2013.

The Navarre Bible: New Testament. New York: Scepter Publishers, 2008.